DNACC ECE

Leading
Early Childhood
Learning Communities

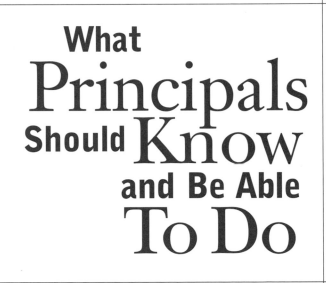

What
Principals
Should Know
and Be Able
To Do

N ESP National Association of Elementary School Principals

Leading Early Childhood Learning Communities was co-created by the National Association of Elementary School Principals and Collaborative Communications Group.

Funds for this publication were generously contributed by Lifetouch Inc., of Minneapolis, MN, Paul Harmel, President and Chief Executive Officer.

National Association of Elementary School Principals

1615 Duke Street
Alexandria, VA 22314-3483
Phone: 800-38-NAESP
Fax: 800-39-NAESP
E-mail: naesp@naesp.org
Web site: www.naesp.org

The mission of NAESP is to lead in the advocacy and support for elementary- and middle-level principals and other education leaders in their commitment to all children

The 30,000 members of the National Association of Elementary School Principals provide administrative and instructional leadership for public and private elementary and middle schools throughout the United States, Canada and overseas. Founded in 1921, NAESP is an independent professional association with its own headquarters building in Alexandria, Virginia. Through national and regional meetings, award-winning publications and joint efforts with its 50 state affiliates, NAESP is a strong advocate for both its members and for the 35 million American children enrolled in preschool, kindergarten and grades 1 through 8.

Vincent L. Ferrandino, Ed.D., Executive Director
Gail Connelly Gross and Deborah B. Reeve, Ed.D., Deputy Executive Directors Cheryl Riggins Newby, Ed.D., Associate Executive Director, Leadership Academy and Urban Alliances

Collaborative Communications Group

1801 Connecticut Avenue NW
Third Floor
Washington, D.C. 20009
Phone: 202-986-4959
Fax: 202-986-4958
E-mail:
info@publicengagement.com
Web site:
www.publicengagement.com

Collaborative Communications Group is a strategic consulting firm that builds the capacity of individuals, organizations and networks to work collaboratively to create solutions that are better than any single entity could produce on its own. Through strategic consulting, dialogue and convening, creation of publications and tools, and community conversations, Collaborative helps organizations and networks to identify, share and apply what they know in ways that increase productivity and effectiveness. The ultimate objective of Collaborative's work is the improvement of the quality of public education and community life.

ISBN 0-939327-22-8

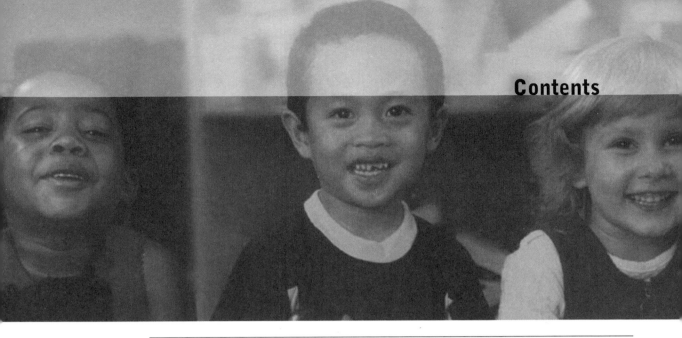

Contents

Foreword by Dr. Vincent Ferrandino

We know that learning begins even before birth. Given the critical nature of learning in the first five years of a child's life, it is imperative that school leaders are actively involved in their communities' early learning programs before students arrive for kindergarten or first grade.

The preschool period begins from birth to school entry at age five. Some 30 percent of all American children begin school unable to maximally profit from the educational experience they will encounter. The percentage is higher for poor children. School readiness is extremely important because nearly every educational benchmark—from being on grade level to staying in school—is related to school readiness.

Public and private support for high-quality early childhood education is growing, and principals of elementary schools need to be ahead of the trend. More than 40 states now provide some funding for pre-K programs, and several are committed to include all children whose parents want to enroll them. Principals across the country are becoming more involved with early childhood programs—leading comprehensive pre-K programs in their school buildings or creating new links with many types of pre-K programs in their communities. Getting to know children and their families long before they enroll in first grade is becoming part of the elementary school principal's responsibility.

High-quality early childhood education is not just an ideal; it's an essential investment. Missed opportunities from birth to school entry can put children behind when they start school and create barriers to achievement that can last through high school. Strong early learning leads to better educated and more employable individuals, as well as less remediation throughout the education system, benefiting all of society. Low-income children stand to gain the most from early childhood education because early intervention helps close achievement gaps and lowers criminal justice costs.

Whether viewed as an issue of equity and fairness or wise public policy, early education is a smart choice: Giving children the right start greatly enhances their opportunities to succeed.

The bar for principal performance continues to rise. *No Child Left Behind*, the Bush administration's education reform act, has increased principals' accountability for student learning. Over the past 15 years, the National Association of Elementary School Principals has partnered with schools, education organizations and policymakers to study, discuss and address new ways to support principals in improving education practice. In the coming years, NAESP will continue to work with innovative individuals and organizations to upgrade practice and culture in schools to reflect what we know about how children learn and develop.

High-quality early childhood education is more than an admirable goal; it is fundamental to making sure all children can reach academic proficiency and achieve intellectual, social and emotional success. It's time to permanently transform our view of the K-12 system to one that starts with pre-kindergarten. Programs need not be school-based, but education leaders should make sure they are school-connected.

This guide will help principals:

• See the need to be strongly involved in learning before kindergarten and first grade. Principals help create the opportunity for high-quality full-day kindergarten and high-quality early childhood education for all students—within public schools or through other early care and education providers in communities. How a full day is defined should be reconsidered. Acknowledging that 60 percent of the mothers of children under six are in the out-of-home workforce, wraparound programs should be provided from 3 p.m. to roughly 6 p.m. to meet the needs of families.

• Recognize that early childhood education is part of the continuum of a child's education because a child's early learning experiences build a foundation for all later learning.

• Create a school culture that values early childhood education. Principals' leadership promotes the important role that early childhood teachers play in providing a foundation for all learning.

- Acknowledge the payoff of effective early interventions, thereby reducing the need for retention or remediation. Well-designed, well-funded interventions can have significant effects on school readiness and subsequent learning outcomes. Research indicates that disadvantaged children seem to benefit more from high-quality early childhood experiences. This suggests that, where budgets are limited, it is appropriate to target early intervention for the most disadvantaged students.

- Understand the importance of properly transitioning children from home into preschool and from preschool into kindergarten. Schools must move beyond sending a single form letter to parents as the sum of an appropriate transition policy.

- See the need for connecting the span of early childhood education that starts with pre-kindergarten and continues until a child begins fourth grade. Principals know that planning is essential to linking all types of early education so that young children have the connections and seamless transitions between pre-K and kindergarten, between kindergarten and first grade, and the important transition from third grade to fourth grade.

- Understand the appropriate role of assessment in pre-K classrooms. Principals familiar with standardized testing and its role in school accountability should understand the limitations of this approach in early learning programs. Assessment in pre-K programs is best when it is led by teachers to help individual children progress and to screen for and diagnose disabilities.

- Acknowledge the role of principal as community leader and promoter of high-quality early childhood education. Principals know they cannot advocate alone for strong early childhood policies, and they value partnerships with non-public school educational programs in the community, including health and fitness advocates and others working to create a web of support and learning for young children.

- Know how to call for school districts, school boards, community leaders, policymakers, parents and educators—from the neighborhood to the national level—to provide the resources necessary to expand the continuum of learning to the vital and productive early years.

Dr. Vincent Ferrandino is the executive director of the National Association of Elementary School Principals.

In 2001, the National Association of Elementary School Principals published *Leading Learning Communities: What Principals Should Know and Be Able To Do*, offering new direction and new thinking for principal leadership. Now, NAESP is releasing a companion guide, *Leading Early Childhood Learning Communities*. This new guide urges elementary school principals to think about where and when learning starts and to support and structure high-quality learning before children reach school in kindergarten or first grade.

This guide is a resource to help principals and others who lead pre-K programs reflect on their work and improve their schools. The guide is also intended for anyone interested in educating young children and improving schools, such as early childhood educators, directors of early childhood programs, school board members, superintendents, professors of education and child development, elementary school teachers and families.

The guide is designed to help principals rethink the connection between early childhood programs and elementary schools. First, NAESP has identified indicators of what we believe constitutes quality in pre-K programs and has defined six standards for what principals must know and be able to do to reach those indicators. The standards cannot be implemented piecemeal; to be successful, principals need to tie them together in the total school program as tightly as possible.

This guide offers practical examples, reflecting the work of principals who helped develop these standards. The Principals' Voices comments come from a group of principals organized for the creation of this guide. Each chapter includes stories of real people in schools that exemplify the guide's recommendations.

Several helpful documents have been included as resources and background. We recognize that readers of this guide work in all kinds of schools, so we listened to principals representing a wide geographic and demographic spectrum to make these materials as useful as possible.

Finally, the guide is designed to encourage reflection. Each standards section includes a list of practical guiding questions principals can ask themselves or a small group at faculty meetings or with grade- or subject-level teams. In addition, each section includes a checklist that leaders of early childhood learning communities can use to assess their own learning and plan next steps.

The Challenge: Expand the Continuum of Learning

Growing knowledge of human development has expanded educational philosophy. Recent brain research makes it clear that children's learning is enhanced by their early childhood experiences. As schools work to ensure that all children develop as proficient students, they need to expand opportunities to include three- and four-year-olds in pre-kindergarten experiences, provide rich full-day kindergarten programs and build new connections to the many early childhood educators across communities.

Rather than simply expecting that young children will be ready to learn when they start kindergarten or first grade, educators are shifting their approach to support children's learning well before they arrive at elementary school.

This guide provides a synthesis of key findings from a rigorous examination of the research on early childhood education. In addition, the guide offers lessons from principals using successful practices in myriad early childhood environments. The objective is to provide useful ideas, practices and tools that can help principals across the country bolster their leadership in pre-K learning.

NAESP's ideal for young children's learning includes programs that are:

- Available to all three-, four- and five-year-olds in every community

- Grounded in sound early childhood development practices like investigation and play

- Guided by ongoing classroom-based assessment, rather than by an over-reliance on norm-referenced testing

- Funded to serve young children well

- Designed to support young children's varied learning needs, languages and cultures

- Part of a continuum of learning that extends from pre-K through third grade with a strong transition to the start of fourth grade

- Operated by schools or other community organizations, with communication and shared expectations between schools and the communities they serve

- Designed to provide full-day options for working families

In many states, the early childhood focus of principals understandably remains on securing funding for full-day kindergarten programs for all children. Even in states at the forefront of offering pre-K programs in schools, many children remain enrolled in programs offered by other providers—churches, community groups, child care centers, Head Start centers and more. Many elementary schools are familiar with the 21st Century Community Learning Centers program, which provides $1 billion for after-school programs for children of elementary school age. The same opportunity should be offered to all preschoolers.

The goal of this guide is not to advocate a formal new step in public schooling: Early childhood education does not need to be based in a school but should be connected to local schools. Elementary school principals should be at the forefront of discussions and activities that reach beyond the elementary campus to make sure everyone involved in pre-K programs—in schools or community settings—understands what it takes for students to be ready to succeed when they reach kindergarten or first grade.

Elementary school principals are in a position to know how many children start school unprepared and the consequences of such learning delays. Elementary principals are also in a key position to define what school readiness means. Therefore, they can serve as leaders in coordinating the array of pre-K programs, making families and pre-K providers aware of what children need to know when they start school and emphasizing the importance of high-quality pre-K learning experiences. By being deeply involved in improving early childhood education, elementary principals help give to children and the entire education system better opportunities to succeed.

Investments in early childhood learning reap significant benefits. A growing body of research, led by the Child-Parent Centers in Chicago, shows a savings of $7 for every dollar invested in pre-kindergarten and other early education programs. Early childhood education helps children to succeed in school and life. Children who finished pre-K programs are half as likely to need special education services in later grades, according to the New York State Department of Education. Other studies have found that children from low-income families who attend high-quality pre-K programs are more likely to graduate from high school and attend college and less likely to go to jail, become teen parents or qualify for welfare. One study even shows that children who attend high-quality pre-K programs also are more likely to own their own home in adulthood.

Even economic leaders have begun to call for high-quality early childhood education. A recent statement from the Committee on Economic Development explains, "Over the past two decades, business leaders have invested time, expertise and resources in efforts to improve K-12 education in the United States. What we have learned leads us to conclude that America's continuing efforts to improve education and develop a world-class workforce will be hampered without a federal and state commitment to early childhood education for three- and four-year-old children."

Six Standards That Characterize Leadership for Early Childhood Learning

As leaders of early childhood learning communities, principals play important roles. They set expectations for learning for young children and they serve as knowledgeable advocates for high-quality early childhood education in schools and into the community.

With the help of principals throughout the association, NAESP identified six standards for what principals should know and be able to do as effective leaders of early childhood learning communities. These actions, taken together, will support young children's learning and improve the schools that serve them.

- Embrace high-quality early childhood programs, principles and practices as the foundation for education throughout the school community

- Engage families and community organizations to support children at home, in the community and in pre-K and kindergarten programs

- Provide appropriate learning environments for young children

- Ensure high-quality curriculum and instructional practices that foster young children's learning and development in all areas

- Use multiple assessments to strengthen student learning and improve the quality of programs

- Advocate for universal opportunity for children to attend high-quality early childhood education programs

Principles of High-Quality Early Childhood Programs

NAESP endorses accreditation criteria for early childhood programs developed by the National Association for the Education of Young Children and professional standards developed by Head Start. NAESP recommends that these criteria guide implementation of all programs, whether they are operated by schools or other community organizations. Based on resources like NAEYC and Head Start Performance Standards, the following principles are just some of the criteria NAESP believes are a necessary resource aligned to the standards in this guide.

This list of indicators is not meant to replace or replicate criteria other organizations have developed that describe high-quality early childhood education programs. This is not an exhaustive list. Indeed, we suggest it as a jumping-off point for principals in their schools and communities to begin to define quality in early childhood programs and to engage in conversations about the quality of early childhood programs where they live. How many of these are present in your school or community? What other indicators might you add?

High-quality early childhood education programs have the following characteristics:

Supportive interactions between teachers and children

The most important indicator of quality is likely to be the nature of the interaction between teacher and child. Indeed, how teachers relate to and interact with children appears to matter more than curriculum in early childhood education.

Teachers facilitate interactions among children to provide opportunities for development of self-esteem, social competence and intellectual growth. Interactions between children and adults allow children to develop an understanding of self and others and are characterized by warmth, personal respect, individuality, positive support and responsiveness.

Safe, supportive and engaging learning environments

Young children learn best in environments that are physically and emotionally safe and that provide opportunities for self-directed learning, exploration and intentional, focused teaching. High-quality programs also reflect the role of play in children's learning and provide environments that encourage play as an important opportunity for children to learn through their own experimentation and exploration. In an early childhood setting, play can be the foundation for building skills in math, literacy, science and other important disciplines.

The health and safety of participants are promoted, and nutritional needs of children and adults are met to promote physical, social, emotional and cognitive development.

Focus on the whole child

A program's approach should include a variety of areas of a child's learning and development, such as the eight factors identified by Head Start, which include: language development, literacy, mathematics, science, creative arts, approaches toward learning, physical health and development and social and emotional development.

The foundation for emotional intelligence is built in early childhood. Emotional intelligence is the ability to understand one's feelings, control impulses and anger, soothe anxiety, show empathy and interact positively with others, and persevere to achieve one's goals. Some research shows that the quality of a child's social skills by age five accurately predicts social and academic competence in later grades.

Meaningful learning for the individual child

Children's approaches to learning—their curiosity, motivation to learn and pride in accomplishment—are keys to success in school achievement and beyond. High-quality programs provide learning experiences that keep these approaches grounded in children's interests and that are developed around themes that unite learning in several disciplines. Teaching reflects the knowledge that young children are active learners, drawing on direct physical and social experience as well as culturally transmitted knowledge to construct their understanding of the world around them.

A culture of authentic assessment and continuous learning

Young children learn and develop at different rates, and their learning cannot be defined by any single assessment. High-quality programs pay attention to all aspects of children's development: physical, social, emotional and intellectual. They are flexible, engaging individual children and supporting their continuous development.

In addition, data helps set direction. Early screenings of children's strengths and learning needs are shared widely—with elementary teachers and leaders of pre-K programs in the community—to strengthen everyone's practice. Finally, systematic assessment of the programs themselves helps ensure that the programs are continually improved.

Connections to families and community organizations

Strong connections to families involve classroom participation, two-way communication and opportunities to incorporate ideas and languages from a child's home and culture into the school environment. Community organizations, such as libraries, recreation centers, clinics and churches, are part of the fabric of young children's lives. Schools that form lasting connections with families and such organizations are better able to support and stimulate a child's development.

Parents feel supported and welcomed as observers and contributors. These pre-K programs are known and valued in their communities. Leaders of educational, civic, cultural, religious and community-based organizations recognize and support schools committed to quality education for young children.

Effective administration

Efficient and effective administration focuses on the needs and desires of children, families and staff. High-quality programs are sufficiently staffed to address and promote children's physical, social, emotional and cognitive development.

Defining Leadership in Early Childhood Education:
Six Standards and Strategies for Principals

STANDARD ONE : Embrace high-quality early childhood programs, principles and practices as the foundation for education throughout the school community.

STRATEGIES

• Consider birth through age eight as a continuum for early learning

• Engage the school community in understanding children's early development and use that combined knowledge to strengthen learning throughout the school

• Balance leadership and management roles to incorporate early childhood programs into the school's culture and organizational structure

• Articulate the value of early intervention to prevent later difficulties

STANDARD TWO: Work with families and community organizations to support children at home, in the community and in pre-K and kindergarten programs.

STRATEGIES

• Acknowledge and support families as children's first and most influential teachers

• Provide early education experiences that are informed by young children's cultural and community experiences

• Act as a bridge between schools and community-based supports for young children and their families

• Build coalitions with community organizations to strengthen learning for children from birth to the start of fourth grade

STANDARD THREE: Provide appropriate learning environments for young children.

STRATEGIES

• Promote environments that are developmentally and age appropriate and address individual ways of learning

• Foster relationships that provide the foundation for children's learning

• Cultivate children's social competencies

• Ensure that facilities and learning opportunities promote children's health and safety

STANDARD FOUR: Ensure high-quality curriculum and instructional practices that foster young children's learning and development in all areas.

STRATEGIES

- Foster young children's eagerness to learn

- Develop early literacy and numeracy skills to provide a foundation for later learning

- Provide ongoing professional development for the school community to build teachers' eagerness to learn

STANDARD FIVE: Use multiple assessments to create experiences that strengthen student learning.

STRATEGIES

- Support teachers in using observation, records and portfolios of student work to demonstrate students' growth

- Use assessments to identify learning barriers and design strategies to overcome them, plan new learning experiences and initiate discussions across grade levels

- Develop systems for sharing information about program effectiveness between school systems and other providers

- Educate parents and report to them on their children's development and individual progress

STANDARD SIX: Advocate for universal opportunity for children to attend high-quality early childhood education programs.

STRATEGIES

- Use the trusted voice of the principal to advocate for the needs of young children in their communities

- Become familiar with early childhood funding streams and policy issues

- Keep the public and policymakers focused on the need for kindergarten programs that match the workday of mothers and fathers and the importance of quality pre-K in a continuum of learning that helps children and schools succeed

Standard One: Embrace Early Childhood Learning

Effective principals embrace high-quality early childhood programs, principles and practices as the foundation for education throughout the school community.

Educators, researchers and policymakers acknowledge the importance of early childhood education for all children before they reach first grade. Research shows that young children have a greater capacity to learn than previously recognized. The first five years of life bring enormous growth in linguistic, cognitive, social and motor skills and emotional competence.

Because children begin learning in infancy, pre-K experiences cannot be seen as separate from education in the early grades.

Effective principals should support an expanded continuum of learning that includes children from age three through the primary grades and a strong transition to the start of fourth grade. Principals provide leadership to build pre-K programs that help children develop the skills necessary to be successful when they enter school in kindergarten or first grade.

By bringing pre-K expectations in line with those in kindergarten and the early school years, principals provide a coherent, related set of experiences for children in the first critical years of schooling.

In schools that cultivate this continuum of learning, early childhood educators are respected for what they can offer their peers in later grades, and teachers in later elementary grades work with pre-K teachers on connecting learning goals and expectations across all levels.

When principals expand the idea of schooling three- and four-year-olds, we see principals who:

- Consider birth through the start of fourth grade a continuum for early learning

- Engage the school community in understanding children's early development and use that combined knowledge to strengthen learning throughout the school

- Balance leadership and management roles to incorporate early childhood programs into the school's culture and organizational structure

- Articulate the value of early intervention to prevent later difficulties

Consider birth through the start of fourth grade a continuum for early childhood learning.

Children are learning even before they are born, and recent advances in brain research underscore the tremendous potential for learning in the early years. Much of children's language learning, for example, takes place before they turn five, the age at which most children enter kindergarten.

Principals who work to enhance pre-K programs serving three- and four-year-olds are making the most of young children's readiness and eagerness for learning. Three-year-olds do not learn in the same ways that third graders do, but they are growing and developing physically and mentally, and they learn from new experiences and develop new skills.

By developing this continuum that sees children through to a strong start in fourth grade, principals demonstrate to the school, community and parents that young children's learning is important.

Many principals have not been trained to be leaders of early childhood programs. In communities where pre-K programs are not a part of the school system, helping connect existing community programs with schools may mean learning about basic early childhood issues and programs and forging new relationships. Even in locales where pre-K programs are located in schools, the need to reach out to other pre-K providers in the community means building new networks of communication and cooperation.

Principals faced with starting a new school-based pre-K program might think about some strategies for creating an early learning community:

- Use a cluster of classrooms in the same part of the school with a shared outdoor play area

- Create an inviting, print-rich environment in rooms and hallways featuring student work and reinforcing early literacy

- Bring teachers together for common planning time to learn from each other

- Work with parents and families of younger students to involve them in the school

- Include young children in events and celebrations at the school

Engage the school community in understanding children's early development and use that combined knowledge to strengthen learning throughout the school.

Young children often learn in informal settings in which the atmosphere is flexible yet meaningful. In pre-K programs, play is a valuable way for children to learn. Singing, for example, develops language skills. Building with blocks builds motor skills and develops spatial awareness. Teachers beyond pre-K and kindergarten should not only recognize the role these activities play but also be aware of the methods of learning that grow from such activity, experience and exploration.

Principals can bridge the gap between pre-K teachers and those in other grades when they encourage all teachers to observe pre-K and kindergarten classrooms to become familiar with the learning that takes place there and understand how early learning builds the foundation for success throughout the elementary school years.

Observing in pre-K classes prompts teachers to think about children's learning and development: Teachers can see firsthand the similarities and differences between children in pre-K and those they teach, and they may gain insight into ways to enhance their own students' learning and development using learning activities adapted from pre-K programs.

Pre-K teachers and kindergarten teachers benefit, too, from observing in primary grade classrooms. They can see the learning that is expected from children there and understand how their work contributes to the learning and development process.

PRINCIPALS' VOICES

"It's important to build a professional learning community at the school. We took the whole staff into the preschool room so they would understand the what and why of children's work there."

Balance leadership and management roles to incorporate early childhood programs into the school's culture and organizational structure.

Much of the principal's work in schools that include very young children continues what good principals already do: managing resources, materials and services to ensure quality and providing leadership that inspires and energizes school staff and others in the community who want to see children achieve at high levels.

There is a growing movement to make high-quality preschool programs available to all three- and four-year-old children. For most pre-K programs, serving additional children without sufficient resources will certainly pose difficult new circumstances. Advocating for additional resources while maintaining high expectations for teachers and students is often an ongoing challenge.

As managers, principals may find that pre-K teachers need a different set of supplies for their classrooms. For example, paints and big brushes may be needed for art projects that help develop coordination and allow children to express ideas and learn to tell stories. Tricycles and other new outdoor equipment may be needed to develop large motor skills. Empty cereal boxes, milk jugs or other food items might be needed to create a grocery store learning center.

Facilities for pre-K programs include specially equipped classrooms with small furniture and easy access to bathrooms and sinks for washing hands, as well as safe and separate areas for outdoor play. Special seating may be necessary in a cafeteria. Because young children often have hands-on learning projects, pre-K classrooms may require more frequent cleaning and take longer to clean than upper-grade classrooms.

Transportation may create additional concerns for principals. Young children are often brought to school and picked up by parents or caregivers. Principals must ensure that children can move from the car to the classroom with as little disruption as possible. Children also need to be kept safely at school until they can be released to a responsible adult. Principals who are visible and accessible when pre-K children are brought to school and picked up can smooth the transition and reassure parents, teachers and students.

At mealtimes, managing space and time and creating an inviting atmosphere for eating is important for young children. Navigating lunch lines can be difficult for them, and a separate time and space for lunch can be helpful. Young children eat more often and schools may need to provide snacks in the morning and afternoon. Adult interaction is valuable at meal and snack time—both for supervision and to promote language development.

Research reveals a connection between high-quality pre-K programs and the experience of program leaders. Principals unfamiliar with exemplary teaching and classroom management practices in pre-K classrooms will want to find opportunities for specialized professional development. Principals should plan to visit a classroom within the district or a neighboring system or visit a classroom in a pre-K program in the community if one is available. Videotapes and other media materials can show effective classroom practices.

PRINCIPALS' VOICES

"I moved parking so that parents could drop off kids or walk them to their classrooms. It seems to promote having more parents in the building. It makes parents feel much better about pre-K."

FOCUS ON PRACTICE

Blending a New Program Into the Heart of the School

Jefferson Elementary School, Norman, Oklahoma

Principal Kathy Taber remembers having a hard time getting fifth-grade teachers to take their hands out of the dry beans in the pre-K sand table.

Taber has been diligent about making sure everyone at Jefferson Elementary is not just aware of the fledgling pre-K program but accepts it as an integral part of the school.

One early step was pulling teachers from pre-K, kindergarten and first grade to plan for faculty training. The whole faculty joined in a session where they came to understand the point of the pre-K program.

"I thought the most damaging thing for the program would be for a teacher to go out in the community and say 'All they do in that four-year-old room is play,'" Taber said, suggesting that people don't understand the importance of play as the most common setting for children's learning.

Pre-K teachers showed fourth- and fifth-grade teachers how blocks help teach spatial concepts and how the sand table, filled with dry beans, was an important learning experience. "They loved it," Taber said.

And when the district studied effects of the pre-K program for a report to the local school board, Taber had the presentation repeated for the Jefferson faculty.

What started as a pilot program at a school where 60 percent of the students qualify for free- or reduced-price lunch has grown both at Jefferson and throughout the district.

Taber, meanwhile, continues to take steps to make pre-K students an obvious part of the life of the 350-student pre-K-5 school.

Pre-K students get weekly time with the physical education and music teachers. After the first two weeks of class, pre-K students join the rest of the students at weekly assemblies.

"Whenever we can, we want to make sure people know that this benefits all our students," Taber said.

Articulate the value of early intervention to prevent later difficulties.

One powerful argument for pre-K programs is their promise in reducing or preventing later difficulties for children, both academic and social. When considering the benefits of pre-K, school staff may think about meeting state and federal academic standards in early elementary school. Families and community members, meanwhile, may look to the longer-term effects of pre-K programs in improving life options, especially for children who live in poverty. Research findings demonstrate that preschool programs, including those in infancy, result in decreases in delinquency and criminality in later years.

Some children enter kindergarten with as few as 4,000 words in their vocabulary while others stretch to 12,000. This disparity reflects their experiences with spoken language. Many children need additional opportunities and support in the pre-K years to create the foundation expected for students starting kindergarten or first grade.

FOCUS ON PRACTICE

Using Pre-K To Start Work on Standards

McFerran Elementary School, Louisville, Kentucky

The 14 pre-K teachers at McFerran Elementary School get a close look at what their students need to know: They spend the first week of every school year helping teach kindergarten.

Principal Carol Miller said that staggering the start of pre-K makes the school run more smoothly, but creating opportunities for pre-K and kindergarten teachers to work together is even more important. It keeps everyone clear about expectations for what students need to know.

"The chance to observe lets teachers get a real feel for curriculum," said Miller, the principal for 25 years.

Kindergarten teachers mentor new pre-K teachers in the building where 350 three- and four-year-olds attend a pre-K center while 600 K-5 students study in an adjacent wing.

Kentucky's education standards spell out what students should know for testing that starts in fourth grade. Many schools have designed their curriculum to trace those skills to kindergarten. The pre-K center at McFerran uses a pre-K curriculum created by the district and connected to state standards.

"There was a time when preschool was focused on socialization—they'd come in, talk about cooperation, take a break, color, rest, and that was it. It's not like that anymore," Miller said. "The expectations are higher. Our kids in kindergarten are reading, which means we want to get our four-year-olds ready for that."

For children still behind after pre-K, Miller encourages parents to sign up for the Pee-Wee Camp that McFerran offers over three weeks in the summer.

Although Miller runs a large school, she spends a good deal of time visiting pre-K classes and sitting in on conferences between pre-K teachers and parents.

"When we started at kindergarten, we'd say if we could get them at four, we could do a better job," she said. "That worked. Now we say we want them at three."

17

The Pre-K Advantage

Researchers have developed several projects to determine whether formal pre-K education makes a long-term difference in children's well-being. Although the exact results and methodology of each study vary, their findings show similar gains for pre-K participants.

The Chicago Child-Parent Centers study results show that:

• Program participants had a 29 percent increase in high school completion rate, including a 47 percent higher rate of school completion for boys

• There was a 33 percent lower rate of juvenile arrests, and a 41 percent lower rate of arrests for violent crimes for the participant group

• For every dollar invested in the preschool program, $7.14 was returned to society in increased earnings for participants and reduced costs for remedial and special education

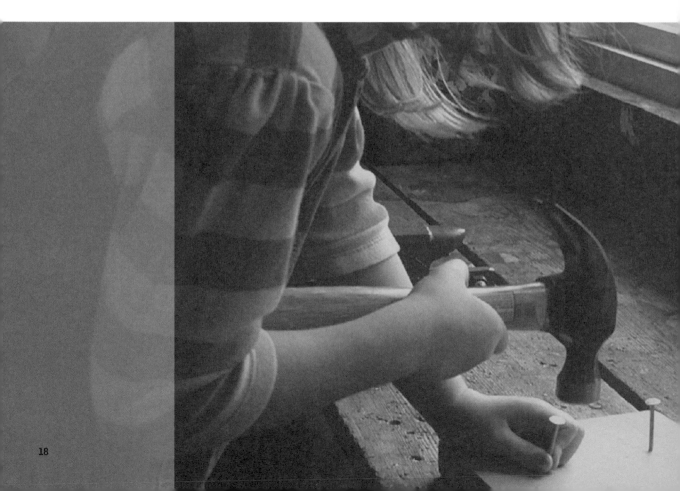

Abecedarian Early Childhood Intervention Project data reveals that:

• 40 percent of program participants versus 20 percent of non-program participants were still in school at age 21

• The project created approximately $4 in benefits for every dollar invested

• Program participants will earn an average of $143,000 more over their lifetimes than will control group members

• School districts saved more than $11,000 per child because participants were less likely to need either special or remedial education

High/Scope Perry Preschool Project results show that:

• The median monthly income of program participants was $1,856 versus a median monthly income of $1,308 for non-program participants

• The program group had significantly fewer lifetime arrests than the non-program group (36 percent versus 55 percent arrested five or more times)

• Every public dollar spent on the program saved $17.07: $12.90 to the general public and $4.17 to each participant

The Oklahoma Universal Pre-K study revealed that:

• Pre-K participants, at the level of kindergarten entry, had higher results on letter-word identification, spelling and applied problem tests than those not exposed to pre-K. Positive gains were made across racial and socioeconomic groups

Questions for Further Reflection

Effective principals embrace high-quality early childhood programs, principles and practices as the foundation for education throughout the school community.

Consider pre-K through the start of fourth grade a continuum for early childhood learning.

Does the vision I've articulated for my school reflect a commitment to early learning? Do the school's organization and practices reflect that vision? How strong are our connections to providers of pre-K services across the community? Am I effective in communicating the vision to parents and members of the community?

Engage the school community in understanding children's early development and use that combined knowledge to strengthen learning throughout the school.

What do we know about young children's development? How do teaching practices throughout the school reflect an understanding of children's development? How can I engage teachers in building an organization focused on children's learning? Does our definition of the school community include all providers of pre-K services in the community?

Balance leadership and management roles to incorporate early childhood programs into the school's culture and organizational structure.

How can I work with pre-K staff to demonstrate my support and expectations for learning? What responsibilities can I share with others? What are the most important leadership challenges I face? What management needs must be met to enable teachers to work effectively with young children?

Articulate the value of early intervention to prevent later difficulties.

What results of pre-K programs can we expect to see among older children at the school? How can I help pre-K teachers meet the needs of all children? Does our school encourage professional discussion among pre-K teachers and teachers of older grades?

Standard One Strategies

Use the Questions for Further Reflection to help you think about and rate the degree to which each Standard One strategy is evident in your school or in your practice as a school leader.

1 Not evident in my school/practice

2 Somewhat or occasionally evident in school/practice

3 Consistently evident in school/practice

4 Consistently evident, with practices that elaborate upon or exceed expectation

Self-Assessment: Beginning of the Year	1	2	3	4
Consider pre-K through the start of fourth grade a continuum for early learning.				
Engage the school community in understanding children's early development and use that combined knowledge to strengthen learning throughout the school.				
Balance leadership and management roles to incorporate early childhood programs into the school's culture and organizational structure.				
Articulate the value of early intervention to prevent later difficulties.				

Notes/Action Steps: Beginning of the Year

Self-Assessment: Middle of the Year	1	2	3	4
Consider pre-K through the start of fourth grade a continuum for early learning.				
Engage the school community in understanding children's early development and use that combined knowledge to strengthen learning throughout the school.				
Balance leadership and management roles to incorporate early childhood programs into the school's culture and organizational structure.				
Articulate the value of early intervention to prevent later difficulties.				

Notes/Action Steps: Middle of the Year

Self-Assessment: End of the Year	1	2	3	4
Consider pre-K through the start of fourth grade a continuum for early learning.				
Engage the school community in understanding children's early development and use that combined knowledge to strengthen learning throughout the school.				
Balance leadership and management roles to incorporate early childhood programs into the school's culture and organizational structure.				
Articulate the value of early intervention to prevent later difficulties.				

Notes/Action Steps: End of the Year

For More Information

On the Web

Frank Porter Graham Institute (www.fpg.unc.edu) publishes a variety of resources about the importance of pre-K programs in preventing academic failure, including information about the Carolina Abecedarian Project.

Center for Research on Children in the United States (www.crocus.georgetown.edu/projects.html) provides an evaluation of Oklahoma's universal pre-K program.

High/Scope Educational Research Foundation (www.highscope.org/Research/PerryProject/perrymain.htm) has published more detailed information about the long-term evaluation of the Perry Preschool Project.

The Annie E. Casey Foundation (www.aecf.org/publications/advocasey/spring2002/chicago.htm) offers additional information on Chicago's Child-Parent Centers.

National Association for the Education of Young Children (www.naeyc.org) provides early childhood education program guidelines and accreditation performance criteria.

Good Start, Grow Smart (www.whitehousegov/infocus/earlychildhood/toc.html) is the Bush Administration's early childhood initiative.

National Institute for Early Education Research (www.nieer.org) supports early childhood education initiatives by providing objective, nonpartisan information based on research. The institute published "A Benefit-Cost Analysis of the Abecedarian Early Childhood Intervention."

From the Research

National Research Council. *Eager To Learn: Educating Our Preschoolers.* Washington, DC: National Academy Press, 2001.

National Research Council and Institute of Medicine. *From Neurons to Neighborhoods: The Science of Early Childhood Development.* Washington, DC. National Academy Press, 2000.

Shore, Rima, *What Kids Need: Today's Best Ideas for Nurturing, Teaching and Protecting Young Children.* Boston, MA: Beacon Press, 2002.

Zigler, Edward. *Head Start and Beyond: A National Plan for Extended Childhood Intervention.* New Haven, CT: Yale University Press, 1995.

Standard Two: Engage Families and Communities

Effective principals work with families and community organizations to support children at home, in the community and in pre-K and kindergarten programs.

Principals know that children begin learning long before they start school. Principals recognize the important role that parents play in their child's development, and they understand that much of a young child's learning takes place outside of school.

Children who are nurtured and encouraged at home are better at forming relationships with adults and peers at school and are better at experiencing solid support for learning. Children who feel the benefits of a supportive community—neighborhoods with safe places to play and relationships that promote social and emotional growth—bring rich experiences and knowledge to their learning.

When young children leave for a classroom and return home, they move between environments in which they may experience different languages, cultures and expectations for behavior. Communication and relationships between home and schools helps to ease transitions and enable children to be comfortable with adults and peers at school.

Nearly one of every five children in the United States is a child of immigrants. Helping these children and their families in the settlement process is an enormous challenge that poses special difficulties for communities and schools. This demands much greater outreach by the schools to other institutions in the community, including the integration of health, employment and other services.

Everyone benefits when communities are able to develop a broad, coherent approach to help families with young children. In most communities, pre-K is an area served by a wide range of programs and providers. Principals should emphasize that while strong pre-K programs need not be based in schools, they would benefit from being connected to elementary schools.

As experts in what schools expect and the goals the education system is working to reach, elementary school principals are in a unique position to take the lead in creating connections between families, educators and providers of community services. Working within the wider community, all providers of pre-K programs should see principals as being focused on the importance of being ready for school and eager to work with others to build new ways to ensure success in the classroom.

Schools that make a special effort to involve parents, offering regular opportunities to meet and discuss a range of education and parenting issues, can help a child's cognitive, social, linguistic and motor development.

Families can also benefit from coordinated community resources to learn more about health, nutrition and fitness programs and how to best support a child with special needs, understand child development or even locate medical, dental and mental health services.

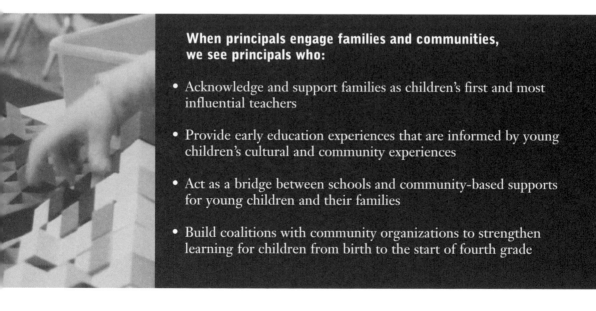

When principals engage families and communities, we see principals who:

- Acknowledge and support families as children's first and most influential teachers

- Provide early education experiences that are informed by young children's cultural and community experiences

- Act as a bridge between schools and community-based supports for young children and their families

- Build coalitions with community organizations to strengthen learning for children from birth to the start of fourth grade

Acknowledge and support families as children's first and most influential teachers.

Young children learn from their parents, guardians or other family members from their earliest days. Principals serve young children best when they honor and build a connection with parents, grandparents and other family members.

When children come to school—at any age—they need to experience a comfortable transition from their home and family. Children should know that their family is welcome at school and that familiar aspects of home, such as language and celebrations, are valued.

Families' attitudes toward school often reflect their own experiences: Those who have had successful experiences may be fairly confident coming to the school or asking questions of teachers, while those who struggled may need assurance that the school values them and their children. Forming partnerships with parents, whatever their previous experience in school, is an important part of maximizing children's opportunities for learning.

Many children who would benefit most from participating in pre-K programs are least likely to be enrolled. Getting children enrolled in pre-K should be a community-wide effort carried out by people who know parents and see them on a regular basis. Principals can help by getting to know people and organizations in their community that work with families, especially organizations serving lower income families or families for whom English is a second language. These families may need additional resources to feel confident in connecting with schools.

Principals who create a seamless support system help parents become involved in and supportive of their children's learning at home and in early education programs. Principals can enlist teachers to help make sure that home-school relationships are positive and strong. Teachers should be encouraged to communicate with parents and support parents' efforts to help their children by:

- Visiting children's homes before the beginning of the school year to meet the children and families. If the parents or the teacher is not comfortable with a home visit, they may decide to meet in a neutral location such as a church or a community facility.

- Creating opportunities for families to visit the pre-K classroom and get acquainted with it before school begins. In some schools, teachers demonstrate learning activities that parents can use at home.

- Encouraging parents as pre-K children make their first transition into a school. Sometimes, starting school is more difficult for an anxious parent than for a child. Principals can help by encouraging parents to have the child stay in the classroom with other students and the teacher, if only for a few minutes at a time. A follow-up call from the principal to assure parents that the child is doing well helps to communicate the school's commitment to welcoming students and parents.

FROM THE FIELD

"Just as high schools have relationships with middle schools and middle schools have relationships with elementary schools, elementary principals must establish relationships with early child care."

Libby Doggett,
Pre-K Now

25

- Reporting to parents on children's experiences on a regular basis. Many experienced pre-K teachers write a weekly note about each child to let parents know what went well and give parents opportunities to support and reinforce progress.

- Establishing and maintaining ongoing communication with all families. To make sure that families are engaged in supporting children's learning, pre-K and kindergarten teachers need to spend more time communicating with parents than those who teach older children. A one-page newsletter or calendar that tells parents what will be happening in the classroom helps extend and reinforce learning by describing the skills students are learning and ways parents can help their children at home. Keeping newsletters centered on learning helps parents stay connected to the school and its expectations and goals.

Principals can also strengthen home-school relationships by promoting a family atmosphere in the pre-K classroom and throughout the school. Young children can learn from a variety of adults, whether they are parents, grandparents or volunteers. High school students and even upper elementary students, for instance, can promote a love of reading and comfort with books when they join the pre-K classroom to read with children. When involving parent volunteers, some may need training and encouragement to be comfortable in the classroom and help build skills like early literacy.

Provide early education experiences that are informed by young children's cultural and community experiences.

Young children come to school from diverse cultural and linguistic backgrounds, and they will learn best in settings that reflect and honor those experiences. Families are often more comfortable when their children's early experiences outside the home reflect the community language, culture and values.

Cultural differences in the way children are brought up—in children's relationships with adults outside the family, for example—can affect children's approaches to learning and their comfort in the classroom. Principals help teachers understand cultural differences and work with children and their families.

In schools in which pre-K programs enroll children from several cultural groups, principals help teachers create a classroom climate that makes all children feel welcome. Pre-K experiences can also help children learn about other cultures through food, art, music and language.

Children's experiences in pre-K programs can also extend their knowledge of the communities in which they live. The community forms a context for learning, and trips to places for learning, like a grocery, post office, library or a park, can build children's sense of connection and belonging to the world outside home and school.

FOCUS ON PRACTICE

Providing a Strong Start To Ensure Quality Results

Endeavour Primary Learning Center, Lauderhill, Florida

Vera Groover, principal of the Endeavour Primary Learning Center thinks long-term: "The object is for our youngsters to go to college," she says. "If we can get it right in preschool, things are going to start working out the way we want them to."

The 70 children enrolled in a special-needs pre-K, Head Start and a state- and county-funded pre-K program get special attention as they start the long path of schooling. Groover and the staff at the school, which has 475 students in grades pre-K-3, feel strongly about seizing the chance to make students' first year a big success.

In addition to efforts the school makes to be inviting and informative to parents—from community events to G.E.D. classes—pre-K teachers make two home visits each year to make a positive first impression on parents, discuss students' accomplishments and needs and talk about any relevant health issues. "We have children who come to our preschool to catch up and get ready for kindergarten. We've realized that work isn't just with the children, it's with their families too," Groover said.

Teachers might talk to parents about the importance of reading with their children and helping them build their vocabulary—even suggesting that on trips to the grocery, they point out how corn is grown or ways potatoes are different from strawberries.

"If we can instill that in preschool, what a difference that makes in our primary grades, and even past that," she said.

Florida's accountability program casts a spotlight on third grade teaching, the first year of statewide testing, as a key point in the elementary grades. Focused on primary and pre-K, Groover sees the key to third-grade success in the experiences of four-year-olds.

"We know that in preschool, what we do impacts everything else," she said.

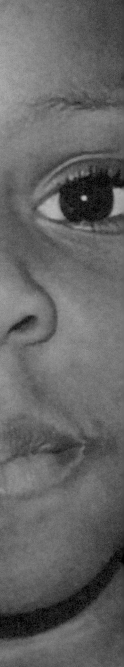

Act as a bridge between schools and community-based supports for young children and their families.

Principals should extend their leadership into the community and make connections with agencies and organizations, seeking supports for children. Teachers may be the first to notice, for instance, that a child is having difficulty paying attention or learning in pre-K programs. Even families that are aware of such conditions may not know how to get help.

When schools begin to enroll young children in pre-K programs, they have a special opportunity to identify problems that can interfere with learning and intervene before children fall behind.

PRINCIPALS' VOICES

"I work with the Child Care Coordinating Committee at the state level. There was no connection with the public schools. We have to work to bridge the two worlds."

Pre-K children may have identified disabilities. Principals need to encourage teachers to meet these students' developmental needs and provide them with opportunities to learn and interact with their non-disabled peers. Teachers should be aware of any additional physical, emotional or learning needs that may arise as children grow and develop. Principals may be able to work with families of children with disabilities to identify resources that will help the school serve such children. Understanding how to appropriately include young children with special needs in a pre-K classroom will likely require additional training or support for teachers.

As principals work to build stronger pre-K connections within the community, they may find connections to other issues, like the need to create wraparound services that help pre-K children and their families get quality services before and after the traditional school day. In many places, schools and child care providers collaborate in providing such services. Principals' outreach to the community and families can grow from presentations to local service clubs, such as Rotary or Kiwanis, or contact with groups of religious leaders to focus on how the entire community can help families.

FOCUS ON PRACTICE

An Isolated School Seeks Help at Every Turn

Roy Elementary School, Roy, Washington

Larry Kuper doesn't have a pre-K program in his school, but that doesn't mean he isn't committed to high-quality early childhood programs. In order to ensure student readiness and success in Roy Elementary School, Kuper reaches out to families to connect them with high-quality pre-K programs in the community.

Reaching out to families in remote Roy, Washington, however, means reaching a long way.

"In a rural area without public transportation, department stores or even a grocery, it's a challenge to connect with the families most in need of support from our schools," said Principal Larry Kuper. "We have to be creative."

About four years ago, Roy Elementary School identified building up its kindergarten program and raising achievement in the early grades as its best shot for meeting state standards. Two years ago, the school district began funding full-day kindergarten at Roy, where scores on introductory kindergarten screenings were the lowest in the district.

Since then, Kuper has been busy building bridges to support the new early childhood emphasis at the 320-student K-6 school where the free- and reduced-price lunch rate is 45 percent. That's meant building community spirit where none has existed.

The school turns every event into an occasion for families. Literacy nights include dinner and an invitation for families to bring all their children. Special activities for three- and four-year-olds help get everyone involved and as familiar as possible with the school's services and expectations. Local pre-K and child-care providers are invited to back-to-school night to meet families and promote their services.

Kuper shares Roy's kindergarten expectations with a nearby day care center and works hand-in-hand with an adjacent pre-K program operated by a local college. He was also recently named to a statewide Child Care Coordinating Committee that advocates for early childhood improvements across Washington State. His experience has helped him work with community agencies: Now a regional mental health services provider works to reach families in Kuper's community and offer services that can help students in the classroom.

"Unless we can start addressing our students' educational needs earlier, we're in an uphill battle," said Kuper, a former primary teacher who has been principal at Roy for seven years. "It's also clear that we need this to be as broad an effort as possible. There are a lot of agencies trying to work for the welfare of kids here—we can't do it as a school or district alone."

Build coalitions with community organizations to strengthen learning for children from birth to the start of fourth grade.

Most schools are relative newcomers to the world of early care and education in their communities. Principals will find a number of groups are already involved, such as:

- Head Start providers or directors, if the school district does not operate Head Start programs in the community

- Early childhood centers, often licensed by the county or state, that provide care for children while their parents are working or in school

- Family child care providers, who usually care for smaller groups of children in their homes

- After-school or wraparound care providers including early childhood centers and other nonprofit organizations like Boys & Girls Clubs of America and churches

- Organizations such as clinics and early intervention services that provide outreach to parents, including home visits to families of children with disabilities

These organizations may meet to share information and effective practice and respond to common challenges such as government requirements. Joining or helping to establish such a coalition can help a principal understand the landscape of programs for young children in the community and identify how schools can best serve children. "Success By 6," for instance, is a United Way program that has created more than 350 community and statewide early childhood coalitions across the country.

In meeting with other early care and early education providers, principals should be aware that the school may be seen as a competitor, especially by family child care providers and centers that serve the entire age range of young children beginning with infants and toddlers.

Principals can play a positive role in coalitions by remaining focused on what is best for children and offering to share resources from the school, such as professional development opportunities. If pre-K programs in the school serve children from working families, principals can help those families establish partnerships with child care centers to care for children during non-school hours. Principals may also be able to create public-private partnerships that offer high-quality pre-K programs within child care facilities.

In some communities, principals meet monthly with local councils made up of agencies and programs that offer family services. As part of the group, principals become aware of families' needs and ways they can be served. In a more specific example of outreach and cooperation between educators and other early childhood service providers, the Wyoming Association of Elementary School Principals hosted one-day workshops on school readiness across the state for early care employees and educators. The $10-per-person workshops drew more than 500 participants.

Mapping Resources for Young Children in Your Community

Principals can help children overcome barriers to learning by connecting them—and their families—with community resources. Involve your school's nurse or social worker (if you have one) in understanding and mapping what is available.

What organizations provide the services this child needs? Public agencies, such as a city or county health department? Private nonprofit organizations with funding to serve some children and their families? Charitable agencies in the community?

Where are they located? How can families get there? Low-income families or new residents may never get across town (or to the next town) unless someone arranges transportation. An appointment won't help if the child can't get there.

Whom do they serve? Some agencies serve only children who are eligible for Medicaid or the state's Children's Health Insurance Program.

Who pays? Some charitable organizations can serve children who do not have health insurance without charging their families.

Getting this information for each child who needs services can be time-consuming. By keeping track of the connections, you can begin to create a map of resources for young children.

Questions for Further Reflection

Effective principals embrace quality early childhood programs, principles and practices as the foundation for education throughout the school community.

Consider pre-K through the start of fourth grade a continuum for early childhood learning.

Does the vision I've articulated for my school reflect a commitment to early learning? Do the school's organization and practices reflect that vision? How strong are our connections to providers of pre-K services across the community? Am I effective in communicating the vision to parents and members of the community?

Engage the school community in understanding children's early development and use that combined knowledge to strengthen learning throughout the school.

What do we know about young children's development? How do teaching practices throughout the school reflect an understanding of children's development? How can I engage teachers in building an organization focused on children's learning? Does our definition of the school community include all providers of pre-K services in the community?

Balance leadership and management roles to incorporate early childhood programs into the school's culture and organizational structure.

How can I work with pre-K staff to demonstrate my support and expectations for learning? What responsibilities can I share with others? What are the most important leadership challenges I face? What management needs must be met to enable teachers to work effectively with young children?

Articulate the value of early intervention to prevent later difficulties.

What results of pre-K programs can we expect to see among older children at the school? How can I help pre-K teachers meet the needs of all children? Does our school encourage professional discussion among pre-K teachers and teachers of older grades?

Standard Two Strategies

Use the Questions for Further Reflection to help you think about and rate the degree to which each Standard Two strategy is evident in your school or in your practice as a school leader.

1 Not evident in my school/practice

2 Somewhat or occasionally evident in school/practice

3 Consistently evident in school/practice

4 Consistently evident, with practices that elaborate upon or exceed expectation

Self-Assessment: Beginning of the Year	1	2	3	4
Acknowledge and support families as children's first and most influential teachers.				
Provide early education experiences that are informed by children's cultural and community experiences.				
Act as a bridge between schools and community-based supports for young children and their families.				
Build coalitions with community organizations to strengthen learning for children from birth to the start of fourth grade.				

Notes/Action Steps: Beginning of the Year

Self-Assessment: Middle of the Year	1	2	3	4
Acknowledge and support families as children's first and most influential teachers.				
Provide early education experiences that are informed by children's cultural and community experiences.				
Act as a bridge between schools and community-based supports for young children and their families.				
Build coalitions with community organizations to strengthen learning for children from birth to the start of fourth grade.				

Notes/Action Steps: Middle of the Year

Self-Assessment: End of the Year	1	2	3	4
Acknowledge and support families as children's first and most influential teachers.				
Provide early education experiences that are informed by children's cultural and community experiences.				
Act as a bridge between schools and community-based supports for young children and their families.				
Build coalitions with community organizations to strengthen learning for children from birth to the start of fourth grade.				

Notes/Action Steps: End of the Year

For More Information

On the Web

Division for Early Childhood (www.dec-sped.org) offers resources such as DEC Recommended Practices: A Comprehensive Guide and the Young Exceptional Children Monograph Series No. 1: Practical Ideas for Addressing Challenging Behavior to help individuals who work with or on behalf of children with special needs, birth through age eight, and their families.

Foundation for Child Development (www.ffcd.org) has a Mapping the PK-3 Continuum (MAP) initiative that supports the restructuring of pre-kindergarten, kindergarten, and grades 1 to 3 into a well-aligned, first level of public education (ages three to eight) in the United States. The foundation has recently launched its New American Children initiative, which aims to stimulate basic and applied research on immigrant children (birth through age 10), particularly those living in low-income families.

Future of Children (www.futureofchildren.org) provides numerous resources for working with young children, including Leveling the Playing Field: Supporting Immigrant Children from Birth to Eight, which provides suggestions for programs to ensure success for immigrant children and their families.

School of the 21st Century (www.yale.edu/21C) presents resources for school-based learning and family support dedicated to the healthy growth and development of all children through coordinated support from birth to age 12. The site also provides research on immigrant children.

Head Start Bureau (www.acf.hhs.gov/programs/hsb/), an arm of the U.S. Department of Health and Human Services, offers a wealth of general information about Head Start, including program performance standards.

Child Care Bureau (www.acf.hhs.gov/programs/ccb/), a federal agency, works with a network of child care providers across the nation.

National Child Care Information Center (www.nccic.org), a service of the Child Care Bureau, is a national clearinghouse and technical assistance center that links parents, providers, policymakers, researchers and the public to early care education information.

United Way of America (national.unitedway.org/sb6) offers information about their Success By 6 network, which works to improve the lives of young children by engaging with multi-sector community partners, including business, health and human services, education, government and community groups.

From the Research

Baker, Amy C., and Lynn Manfredi-Petitt, *Relationships, the Heart of Quality Care: Creating Community Among Adults in Early Care Settings.* Washington, DC: National Association for the Education of Young Children, 2004.

Dryfoos, Joy, and Sue Maguire, *Inside Full-Service Community Schools.* Thousand Oaks, CA: Corwin Press, 2002.

Epstein, Joyce L., *School, Family and Community Partnerships: Preparing Educators and Improving Schools.* Boulder, CO: Westview Press, 2001.

Pianta, Robert C., and Marcia Kraft-Sayre, *Successful Kindergarten Transition: Your Guide to Connecting Children, Families and Schools.* Baltimore, MD: Brookes Publishing Co., 2003.

Standard Three: Promote Appropriate Learning Environments for Young Children

Effective principals recognize the role of rich learning environments for young children and help create them.

For young children, learning takes place on many levels at once: While painting a picture at an easel, a young child practices both small- and large-muscle coordination, learns the names of colors and what happens when they are mixed and uses imagination and language to describe events and emotions expressed by their creation.

Beyond gaining from those new experiences, children in the pre-K years also are constantly building knowledge from the physical and social world swirling around them.

Relationships are a particular source of learning in the early years, with children drawing knowledge from the connections between staff members and children, among adults in the classroom, among children in groups and between children and the activities they encounter.

There are two types of variables in a setting: structural variables (such as group size, child/staff ratio, etc.) and process variables (such as the nature and quality of interactions between the child and the teacher). Infant child care research from the National Institute of Child Health and Human Development indicates that one set of variables is not more important than the other. Good structural variables (such as fewer children per teacher) can make process variables (such as more supportive interactions between teacher and child) possible. Principals use their leadership and management skills to ensure appropriate environments when they observe and analyze interactions in the classroom and provide feedback as well as tailoring materials, schedules and space to pre-K learning.

When the interpersonal and physical learning environments are stimulating and supportive, children are able to develop in many ways. Principals recognize the key role of rich learning environments for young children and provide leadership in creating them.

When principals support and promote appropriate learning environments for young children, we see principals who:

- Promote environments that are developmentally and age appropriate and address individual ways of learning

- Create relationships that provide the foundation for children's learning

- Develop children's social skills

- Provide facilities and learning opportunities that promote children's health and safety

Promote environments that are developmentally and age appropriate and address individual ways of learning.

A developmentally appropriate classroom addresses four components of pre-K learning—knowledge, skills, attitudes and feelings.

Principals support developmentally appropriate practices in early childhood education programs by helping teachers interact with children in ways that promote and extend learning for every child. Although developmentally appropriate classroom environments have an underlying structure, it may not be apparent to a casual visitor. Principals who spend time in the classroom should be able to see how each activity is related to aspects of child development and how it's aligned with early learning curriculum goals.

Classroom activities guided by individual children's interests and choices often have an overall theme that stimulates children's curiosity and frames learning. Activity centers, or learning centers, in the classroom build on children's development. They allow opportunities for play to promote language and social development; projects and building blocks to develop hand skills; story time for language development; experiences in measuring and comparing sizes to stimulate thought and questioning, all during a single session.

In pre-K classrooms, play leads to exploration and hands-on experiences. This not only helps a child interact with their environment but also encourages abstract thought and creativity. Play is an important aspect of pre-K learning experiences; principals need to be able to clearly explain how young children learn through play.

Small and large group activities and activities chosen by preschool children provide high-quality learning opportunities. Time in a circle with teachers and other children builds social skills and language development. In classrooms designed for pre-K chil-

Age appropriate practices reflect what is known about child development and learning based on human development during an age span. Development includes children's movement, hand and finger skills, language, cognitive, social, cultural and emotional development. An understanding of human development guides planning for the learning environment and activities in early childhood. Activities that require following a four-step sequence, for example, may not be appropriate for most three-year-olds, who usually are able to respond to two- or three-step requests.

Individually appropriate practices reflect what is known about the strengths, interests and needs of a particular child in the group, adapting and responding to individual conditions. Both disabilities and experiences are likely to affect individual development. For example, a child with a hearing disability may not meet age-appropriate expectations for language development, such as speaking in four- or five-word sentences, while a child who has not used crayons or markers may have difficulty holding a pencil in a writing position, another expectation for three-year-olds.

dren, teacher-led lessons and whole-group activities are limited. Children's interests and choices guide the learning experiences, and teachers and other adults are likely to interact with children individually or in small groups.

Activities are attuned to children's development, recognizing the shorter attention spans and limited social skills of some young children. As children mature, more structured activities may be introduced. Over time, as children learn and mature, principals should see changes in the structure and activities in developmentally appropriate classrooms as well as changes in children's behavior and skills. The importance of these kinds of experiences also point to the need for pre-K teachers with specialized training in working with young children.

Create relationships that provide the foundation for children's learning.

Next to their parents, teachers are often the most important people in young children's lives. Children need to be able to trust their teachers and feel safe and accepted in order to learn. Successful pre-K classrooms are warm, inviting places where children have ongoing opportunities for learning. Adults guide and encourage children to stretch what they know by trying new things.

Positive, nurturing relationships between teachers and students develop when class sizes are kept small and classroom activities are organized to allow teachers to spend individual time with each child every day.

The National Association for the Education of Young Children advises that two teachers with specialized training work with children in groups of six to eight for infants, groups of 10 to 12 for two- and three-year-olds, and groups of 16 to 20 for four- and five-year-olds. Most states have their own class-size rules. In Oklahoma, for example, schools with pre-K classes with more than 15 students must have an assistant, and capacity for any pre-K class is 20.

Younger children require more individual attention. Pre-K teachers need to be able to sit alongside a child—or offer a lap—to create a sense of physical closeness and trust, especially when introducing new concepts or working in areas where children are putting new skills to the test.

Develop children's social and emotional skills.

Social and emotional learning is important for pre-K children, who are starting to form and maintain positive relationships with peers and adults. Children learn through relationships, and many child development experts believe that gaining social skills in early childhood is the key to being able to form and maintain positive relationships throughout life.

Principals help teachers organize pre-K learning environments so children can learn to share, to talk and listen to each other, to ask and respond to questions, and to share ideas and experiences in a group. This social and emotional learning lays the groundwork for children to pay attention and participate in more academic learning as they grow.

Principals also help teachers respond to children's challenging behaviors. Many young children may hit, kick, throw tantrums or use inappropriate language at times during their early development to get their needs met or deal with their frustrations. For most, the behavior is short-term and decreases as they learn socially acceptable ways of asking for help or expressing their needs.

For some children, however, challenging behaviors becomes more consistent and disruptive. Their behavior keeps them from learning and affects their classmates' learning. They may present a physical danger to themselves or to others. Overcoming these behaviors is important for success in more formal classrooms at kindergarten and later grades.

For children whose behavior continues to interfere with their learning and social relationships, principals can encourage teachers to adopt strategies that have been shown to be effective for young children. The Center for Evidence-Based Practice for Young Children With Challenging Behavior has produced a synthesis of intervention procedures for young children that can help teachers intervene in a way that will help children overcome inappropriate behavior.

Principals play a key role in helping teachers and families work with children who exhibit challenging behaviors. They help teachers develop classroom management skills that reduce these behaviors, such as planning carefully for transitions between activities. Principals also serve as a bridge between school and home so that parents and teachers work together to carry out a plan to improve behavior.

Families play a critical role in designing and carrying out interventions for challenging behavior and should be engaged from the beginning in planning. Children are more likely to be able to improve their behavior when they experience an approach that is consistent between school and home.

FOCUS ON PRACTICE

Engaging Students in Learning

Anna Silver School for Technology and the Arts, New York, New York

Leonard Golubchick has been principal of P.S. 20, the Anna Silver School for Technology and the Arts, since 1978. Throughout its history, the school has served immigrant families who came to New York from all over the world.

The school now enrolls 882 students in grades pre-K-6; for 65 percent, English is a second language, and 20 percent qualify for special education services. The New York Times described P.S. 20 as "one of the poorest schools in America, but also one of the most thrilling." In recent years, the school's scores on state-mandated tests have improved so much that the state education commissioner wrote students a congratulatory letter.

The secret, says Golubchick, is engaging children, even the youngest ones, in the process of learning.

"Children have to be able to tell us the process," he says. "What are you learning? How are you learning?" To involve students and stimulate learning, teachers use themes that weave together science, social studies, math and the arts. Golubchick secured other resources to be able to offer rich and varied learning experiences, beginning with pre-K. For example, students use a multi-purpose space in the school to simulate the streets of their community and learn about the work of people in the community.

Golubchick said the school can improve students' learning by analyzing data that's often already at their fingertips. "When kindergarten students walk in the door," he says, "they get multiple assessments. We have to think about the structure for learning that the results suggest." He insists that teachers pay attention to curriculum, instruction and assessment and keep raising the bar for student learning.

Golubchick offers advice for elementary school principals who want to improve children's learning: "Understand children's development, bridge home and school and advocate for quality universal pre-K with trained personnel, possibly in public schools."

Provide facilities and learning opportunities that promote children's health and safety.

During pre-K years, children learn basic routines that will last a lifetime. Health and safety are key components of pre-K learning environments. Children are often taught hand-washing and other routines that reduce the spread of contagious disease. When principals place a pre-K program in a traditional elementary classroom, they need to follow local and district guidelines for these rooms, such as storage areas for materials that may be harmful to children, easy access to child-sized bathroom facilities and secure locks on windows and areas where children are not allowed to play. Classroom and outside environments must allow for children to be under adult supervision at all times.

Principals also ensure that pre-K programs incorporate adequate time for children to be physically active. Recent findings about the increase in childhood obesity link it to reduced physical activity. Pre-K practices can have a lasting influence on children's activity levels, and these levels can vary greatly among pre-K programs.

Pre-K children need opportunities for physical activity during school, with outdoor time when the weather permits and opportunities for movement and motor development. Children's balance also is an important part of physical development and learning that should be incorporated into pre-K programs.

FOCUS ON PRACTICE

Tailoring Teaching to Student Needs

Greenridge Elementary School, Comstock Park, Michigan

Principal Stacy Stoll takes pride as she explains that Greenridge Elementary School in Comstock Park, Michigan, is a work in progress: Teachers are always thinking about what works and reinventing their approach to adapt to the shifting needs of students at the pre-K-kindergarten school.

"Creating a nurturing, safe, engaging environment is at the heart of everything we do," Stoll said, "but we're always looking for new things that explain young ones and how we can help them learn at increased rates."

To create a positive learning environment for students, the principal focuses on making sure teachers keep learning, too—in faculty meetings, book study groups and daily conversations.

Teachers have studied multiple intelligences and brain research findings and used what they learned to update their curriculum and teaching. They've also made changes on the go: Last year, when significantly more boys than girls enrolled and teachers' frustration over disruptive behavior grew, the faculty jumped into action.

"We spent a lot of time as a staff finding out about ways boys learn differently than girls," Stoll recalled. "We let the kids stand up and move around more during lessons and switched to a phonics program with more movement."

Stoll, a fifth-year principal at the 380-student school, said that an awareness that students in the pre-K years are so ripe for learning helps underscore the need for the staff to be open to change and eager to learn.

Meetings about new concepts such as giving students more choice in what they learn quickly lead to very practical questions: "Our professional discussions involve asking whether what we learn means we're going to do something different to engage our kids," Stoll said.

Head Start Performance Standards

The following language is excerpted from federal regulations revised on Oct. 1, 2004. The official citation is 45CFR1304.21.

In order to help children gain the skills and confidence necessary to be prepared to succeed in their present environment and with later responsibilities in school and life, grantee and delegate agencies' approach to child development and education must:

- Be developmentally and linguistically appropriate, recognizing that children have individual rates of development as well as individual interests, temperaments, languages, cultural backgrounds and learning styles

- Be inclusive of children with disabilities, consistent with their Individualized Family Service Plan or Individualized Education Program

- Provide an environment of acceptance that supports and respects gender, culture, language, ethnicity and family composition

- Provide a balance of child-initiated and adult-directed activities, including individual and small group activities

- Allow and enable children to independently use toilet facilities when it is developmentally appropriate and when efforts to encourage toilet training are supported by the parents

Parents must be:

- Invited to become integrally involved in the development of the program's curriculum and approach to child development and education

- Provided opportunities to increase their child-observation skills and to share assessments with staff that will help plan the learning experiences

- Encouraged to participate in staff-parent conferences and home visits to discuss their child's development and education

Grantee and delegate agencies must support social and emotional development by:

- Encouraging development which enhances each child's strengths by building trust; fostering independence; encouraging self-control by setting clear, consistent limits and having realistic expectations; encouraging respect for the feelings and rights of others; and supporting and respecting the home language, culture and family composition of each child in ways that support the child's health and well-being

- Planning for routines and transitions so that they occur in a timely, predictable and unrushed manner according to each child's needs

Grantee and delegate agencies must provide for the development of each child's cognitive and language skills by:

- Supporting each child's learning, using various strategies including experimentation, inquiry, observation, play and exploration

- Ensuring opportunities for creative self-expression through activities such as art, music, movement and dialogue

- Promoting interaction and language use among children and between children and adults

- Supporting emerging literacy and numeracy development through materials and activities according to the developmental level of each child

In center-based settings, grantee and delegate agencies must promote each child's physical development by:

- Providing sufficient time, indoor and outdoor space, equipment, materials and adult guidance for active play and movement that support the development of gross motor skills

- Providing appropriate time, space, equipment, materials and adult guidance for the development of fine motor skills according to each child's developmental level

- Providing an appropriate environment and adult guidance for the participation of children with special needs

In home-based settings, grantee and delegate agencies must encourage parents to appreciate the importance of physical development, provide opportunities for children's outdoor and indoor active play and guide children in the safe use of equipment and materials.

Grantee and delegate agencies' program of services for infants and toddlers must encourage:

- The development of secure relationships in out-of-home care settings for infants and toddlers by having a limited number of consistent teachers over an extended period of time. Teachers must demonstrate an understanding of the child's family culture and, whenever possible, speak the child's language

- Trust and emotional security so that each child can explore the environment according to his or her developmental level

- Opportunities for each child to explore a variety of sensory and motor experiences with support and stimulation from teachers and family members

Grantee and delegate agencies must support the social and emotional development of infants and toddlers by promoting an environment that:

- Encourages the development of self-awareness, autonomy and self-expression

- Supports the emerging communication skills of infants and toddlers by providing daily opportunities for each child to interact with others and to express himself or herself freely

Grantee and delegate agencies must promote the physical development of infants and toddlers by:

- Supporting the development of the physical skills of infants and toddlers, including gross motor skills such as grasping, pulling, pushing, crawling, walking and climbing

- Creating opportunities for fine motor development that encourage the control and coordination of small, specialized motions, using the eyes, mouth, hands and feet

In providing child development and education for preschoolers, grantee and delegate agencies, in collaboration with the parents, must implement a curriculum that:

- Supports each child's individual pattern of development and learning

- Provides for the development of cognitive skills by encouraging each child to organize his or her experiences, to understand concepts, and to develop age appropriate literacy, numeracy, reasoning, problem solving and decision-making skills, which form a foundation for school readiness and later school success

- Integrates all educational aspects of the health, nutrition and mental health services into program activities

- Ensures that the program environment helps children develop emotional security and facility in social relationships

- Enhances each child's understanding of self as an individual and as a member of a group

- Provides each child with opportunities for success to develop feelings of competence, self-esteem and positive attitudes toward learning

- Provides individual and small group experiences, both indoors and outdoors

Pre-K teachers should use a variety of strategies to promote and support children's learning and developmental progress based on the observations and ongoing assessment of each child.

Overview of the Major Categories in the Early Childhood Environment Rating Scale

The Early Childhood Environment Rating Scale lists important parts of a good learning environment for young children. It includes 43 areas that can be assessed by trained observers in the classroom. A summary of the list, below, allows principals to think about important general categories in creating a strong environment for early learning.

Space and Furnishings

- Indoor space
- Furniture for routine care, play and learning
- Furnishings for relaxation and play
- Room arrangement for play
- Space for privacy
- Child-related display
- Space for gross motor play
- Gross motor equipment

Personal Care Routines

- Greeting/departing
- Meals/snacks
- Nap/rest
- Toileting/diapering
- Health practices
- Safety practices

Language and Reasoning

- Books and pictures
- Encouraging children to communicate
- Using language to develop reasoning skills
- Informal use of language

Activities

- Fine motor
- Art
- Music/movement
- Blocks
- Sand/water
- Dramatic play
- Nature/science
- Math/numbers
- Use of TV, video and/or computers
- Promoting acceptance of diversity

Interaction

- Supervision of gross motor activities
- General supervision of children
- Discipline
- Staff-child interactions
- Interactions among children

Program Structure

- Schedule
- Free play
- Group time
- Provisions for children with disabilities

Parents and Staff

- Provisions for parents
- Provisions for personal needs of staff
- Staff interaction and cooperation
- Supervision and evaluation of staff
- Opportunities for professional growth

Questions for Further Reflection

Effective principals embrace quality early childhood programs, principles and practices as the foundation for education throughout the school community.

Consider pre-K through the start of fourth grade a continuum for early childhood learning.

Does the vision I've articulated for my school reflect a commitment to early learning? Do the school's organization and practices reflect that vision? How strong are our connections to providers of pre-K services across the community? Am I effective in communicating the vision to parents and members of the community?

Engage the school community in understanding children's early development and use that combined knowledge to strengthen learning throughout the school.

What do we know about young children's development? How do teaching practices throughout the school reflect an understanding of children's development? How can I engage teachers in building an organization focused on children's learning? Does our definition of the school community include all providers of pre-K services in the community?

Balance leadership and management roles to incorporate early childhood programs into the school's culture and organizational structure.

How can I work with pre-K staff to demonstrate my support and expectations for learning? What responsibilities can I share with others? What are the most important leadership challenges I face? What management needs must be met to enable teachers to work effectively with young children?

Articulate the value of early intervention to prevent later difficulties.

What results of pre-K programs can we expect to see among older children at the school? How can I help pre-K teachers meet the needs of all children? Does our school encourage professional discussion among pre-K teachers and teachers of older grades?

Standard Three Strategies

Use the Questions for Further Reflection to help you think about and rate the degree to which each Standard Three strategy is evident in your school or in your practice as a school leader.

1 Not evident in my school/practice

2 Somewhat or occasionally evident in school/practice

3 Consistently evident in school/practice

4 Consistently evident, with practices that elaborate upon or exceed expectation

Self-Assessment: Beginning of the Year	1	2	3	4
Promote environments that are developmentally and age appropriate and address individual ways of learning.				
Create relationships that provide the foundation for children's learning.				
Develop children's social competency.				
Provide facilities and learning opportunities that promote children's health and safety.				

Notes/Action Steps: Beginning of the Year

Self-Assessment: Middle of the Year	1	2	3	4
Promote environments that are developmentally and age appropriate and address individual ways of learning.				
Create relationships that provide the foundation for children's learning.				
Develop children's social competency.				
Provide facilities and learning opportunities that promote children's health and safety.				

Notes/Action Steps: Middle of the Year

Self-Assessment: End of the Year	1	2	3	4
Promote environments that are developmentally and age appropriate and address individual ways of learning.				
Create relationships that provide the foundation for children's learning.				
Develop children's social competency.				
Provide facilities and learning opportunities that promote children's health and safety.				

Notes/Action Steps: End of the Year

For More Information

On the Web

Center for Evidence-Based Practice: Young Children with Challenging Behavior (challengingbehavior.fmhi.usf.edu) offers a synthesis of intervention procedures for young children that helps teachers determine how to help children overcome inappropriate behavior.

Center on the Social and Emotional Foundations for Early Learning (www.cse-fel.uiuc.edu) offers evidence-based, user-friendly information to help early childhood educators meet the needs of the growing number of children with challenging behaviors and mental health challenges in child care and Head Start programs.

National Association for the Education of Young Children (www.naeyc.org) has produced Tools for Teaching Developmentally Appropriate Practice, videos that demonstrate excellent teaching in a wide range of programs including infant/toddler rooms, child care centers, pre-K, family day care homes, kindergartens and primary grade classrooms. Videos are available from NAEYC.

National Institute of Child Health and Human Development (www.nichd.nih.gov), part of the National Institutes of Health, supports and conducts research on topics related to the health of children, adults, families and populations.

National Institute for Early Education Research (www.nieer.org) supports early childhood education initiatives by providing objective, nonpartisan information based on research. The institute published "A Benefit-Cost Analysis of the Abecedarian Early Childhood Intervention."

Frank Porter Graham Center (www.fpg.unc.edu) describes the Early Childhood Environment Rating Scale in more detail, as well as other rating scales for infant/toddler programs and family childcare settings. The center also offers information about publications and training.

Education Week (www.edweek.org) reports regularly on pre-K issues.

From the Research

Bell, Susan Hart, Victoria W. Carr, Dawn Denno, Lawrence J. Johnson and Louise R. Phillips. *Challenging Behaviors in Early Childhood Settings: Creating a Place for All Children.* Baltimore, MD: Brookes Publishing Co., 2004.

Bredekamp, S. and Carol Copple, Eds. *Developmentally Appropriate Practice in Early Childhood Programs.* Washington, DC: National Association for the Education of Young Children, revised 1997.

Zigler, E. F., D. G. Singer and S. J. Bishop-Josef, Eds. *Children's Play: The Roots of Reading.* Washington, DC: Zero to Three Press, 2004.

Standard Four: Ensure Quality Teaching

Effective principals ensure high-quality curriculum and instructional practices that foster young children's learning and development.

In a developmentally appropriate classroom, the curriculum strives to help children become lifelong learners, think critically and imaginatively, ask meaningful questions, formulate alternative solutions, appreciate diversity and work collaboratively. Perhaps most important, quality teaching can help build a child's capacity to form meaningful relationships with others.

People learn by making connections. Ultimately, the objective of high-quality teaching is to make learning meaningful for the individual child, using practices that reflect both the age and the needs of a student.

Author Bob Sornson writes in Preventing Early Learning Failure that three basic ideas govern teaching children so that they can be successful in school:

- **Not all children are ready for instruction at the same level when they come to school.** Expecting all young children to learn from the same materials at the same rate is not going to work.

- **All important basic skills should be learned completely, until the concepts seem simple and easy to use.** Children should understand fundamental concepts and skills so well that they become embedded in what children know and can do.

- **If we want a child to use a skill throughout life, it must be associated with joy.** Children who are glad to learn to read will choose to read on their own. Forcing students to practice tasks in frustration guarantees that they will avoid doing them in the future.

49

When principals work to ensure high-quality teaching in the pre-K classroom, we see principals who:

- Foster young children's eagerness to learn

- Develop early literacy and early numeracy skills to provide a foundation for later learning

- Provide ongoing professional development for the school community to build an eagerness to learn

Foster young children's eagerness to learn.

Lilian Katz of the Early Childhood and Parenting Collaborative at the University of Illinois writes that at every level of education and for every subject, there are three important goals: the acquisition of knowledge; the acquisition of skills and the development of the dispositions to use them. In the pre-K years, knowledge refers to a variety of facts, concepts, ideas, stories, rhymes and routines that can be known and understood at a young age.

Dispositions can be thought of as habits of the mind. An easy example is curiosity. While difficult to teach, developing curiosity is significant to learning and can be supported and strengthened throughout childhood.

Getting in the right frame of mind for learning is as important as academics in pre-K. Academics are important, as is an inborn desire to master problems presented by the environment. As some skills or areas prove difficult for some young children, an eagerness to learn may carry a child through the struggle and help keep him or her motivated.

Research shows that while teacher-led instruction can produce short-term results, staying focused on intellectual development is the best route to long-term academic success. Principals can help guard against focusing on too much academic instruction too soon with pre-K children. Keeping the lifelong benefits of quality pre-K programs in mind—increased chances of graduating from high school and moving into postsecondary education—principals can help teachers and parents avoid focusing on short-term academic goals to the detriment of a developing an intellect turned on to learning.

Develop early literacy and early numeracy skills to provide a foundation for later learning.

Research portrays the human brain as a pattern detector that works best when processing meaningful material—a critical reason to tie literacy, numeracy, science, social studies and other new skills to experiences in a child's life. As in real life, curriculum in pre-K classrooms crosses subject-area boundaries through learning and activity centers built around themes. These themes and projects link content from various topics to show connections across disciplines.

Language acquisition is crucial in developing the intellectual ability of a young child. Language, social and cognitive development are essential aspects of each other. Mastering oral language is regarded as the most significant milestone in children's cognitive development. Language does not merely reflect thought; it provides a way to understand and interpret experience.

Recent research points to critical periods in development when the learning environment can influence how an individual's brain is "wired" for functions such as math, language, music and physical activity. If these windows of opportunity are missed—if the brain does not receive the appropriate stimulation during a critical period—it is more difficult for the brain to rewire itself at a later stage of development. For example, children can learn new languages more quickly at early ages than when they are older, leading some advocates to say it would be more productive to teach new languages in elementary grades than in high school.

Numeracy refers to a child's capacity for quantitative thought and expression. To grasp how numbers apply to real life, children are given many opportunities for

hands-on experiences with pegboards, blocks, number lines and materials for counting and measuring. Rather than memorizing isolated facts and rules, children actively participate in their learning, inventing their own procedures for solving computation and story problems.

Rather than being thought of as a set of skills and procedures that children must acquire, mathematics in a pre-K setting is the search for order and pattern in the world around us. Early numeracy, then, is not simply the foundation of math; it's fundamental to all learning.

In addition to learning basics of language and numbers, children's learning experiences should also help build foundations in areas like science, geography, economics, the arts, health and more. Teachers in pre-K classrooms should see connections between disciplines and how skills like knowing the difference between solids and liquids in science can be helpful in distinguishing triangles from squares in math.

Provide ongoing professional development for the school community to foster children's eagerness to learn.

Teachers and others in schools often feel pressure to achieve quick academic gains for children, such as reaching specific standards in kindergarten or first grade. Principals are responsible for creating a climate throughout the school that carefully balances children's intellectual growth and cultivate habits for learning as well as reaching academic mileposts.

Principals take the lead by emphasizing professional development that creates learning communities in which teachers meet regularly to discuss common challenges and share effective practice. Principals stimulate teachers' intellectual growth by choosing challenging topics for professional development and making every activity an opportunity to learn.

Principals are responsible for creating a climate throughout the school that carefully balances children's intellectual growth and cultivate habits for learning as well as reaching academic mileposts. In the learning community, teachers begin by identifying their own learning styles and those of other staff and extend that tailor their teaching to children's ways of learning.

FOCUS ON PRACTICE

Laying the Groundwork for Reading Success

All Ready Preschool, Paradise Valley Elementary School, Casper, Wyoming

Learning takes many forms at the All Ready Preschool at Paradise Valley Elementary School.

The program, started 10 years ago by two teachers who wanted to see if early interventions could enhance students' readiness for kindergarten, focuses on at-risk children ready for pre-K.

Small literacy groups meet every day for three to 12 minutes. Some three-year-olds may sit on a teacher's lap turning pages of a book and discussing pictures. Another group might work with a volunteer parent or aide identifying letters in their names, while another works through a rhyming activity.

Principal Christine Frude sees the pre-K classroom as a nurturing environment in which students reach their own developmental levels. "Every single day, there should be some instruction provided in each child's own learning zone," Frude said.

Targeting students who are not eligible for Head Start, the half-day sessions at the pre-K-6 school combine play with other learning experiences that build early literacy skills.

"There are sand and water tables, dramatic play centers, art and science centers, but every day we do things with our preschoolers that we'd teach or show our own children to help them learn," she said. "We try to find out what each child already knows or has an understanding of and link their learning to it."

Frude closely monitors the program's effects at the 430-student school in which 46 percent of the students qualify for free- or reduced-price meals. Most important, she said, the children don't start kindergarten behind. An unexpected benefit: The rate of students identified with learning disabilities has dropped by 50 percent.

Ensuring the First Steps Toward Academic Success

Rossmoor Elementary School, Los Alamitos, California

The pre-K program at Rossmoor Elementary School is run by the school district and operates with a full-time director. But Rossmoor principal Laurel A. Telfer doesn't see that as a reason not to be deeply involved in the program housed in her 600-student school.

As Rossmoor's instructional leader, she observes the 24 students in the school's pre-K Child Development Center and makes sure that what they learn lines up with California's early readiness standards and the state's curriculum standards for kindergarten. She meets regularly with the program director to talk about ways to plan and measure what students need to know before they move on to kindergarten.

"We make sure that one skill leads into another," Telfer said. "I send our kindergarten teachers in to observe. It's all part of a conscious effort to bring together everybody to make sure what we do is connected."

She said that California's efforts to define what pre-K students need to know help. The state has also offered developmental guidelines that help principals and pre-K teachers think about how students are learning.

When teachers ask students to clean off a tabletop and then get their coats, Telfer recognizes that the young children are showing whether they can accomplish two-step tasks that are sequential but not related. Other skills, like whether children can create their own rhymes, are monitored by teachers who know that's one of the first steps in an academic plan that will continue throughout the elementary grades and beyond.

"Schools need to have a continuum of learning, and the more focused we can be with resources and parental involvement early on, the more we'll see success," said Telfer, a principal for 14 years. "It really takes very little on my part to sit in those classes, observe what they're doing and make sure it's aligned with what we're trying to do."

Sample Pre-K Learning Standards

Several states have adopted standards or curriculum guidelines that spell out what children in pre-K programs should know and be able to do. Below is a sample of the language and content that guide pre-K learning experiences to prepare students for kindergarten in two states.

OKLAHOMA

Oral Language

The child will listen for information and for pleasure.

- Listens with interest to stories read aloud

- Understands and follows oral direction

  The child will express ideas or opinions in group or individual settings

- Uses language for a variety of purposes (e.g., expressing needs and interests)

- Recalls and repeats simple poems, rhymes and songs

- Uses sentences of increasing length (three or more words) and grammatical complexity in everyday speech

- Shares simple personal narrative

- Participates actively in conversations

Literacy

Print Awareness: The child will understand the characteristics of written language.

- Demonstrates an awareness of concepts of print

- Identifies the front cover and back cover of a book

- Follows book from left to right and from top to bottom on the printed page

- Begins to recognize the relationship or connection between spoken and written words by following the print as it is read aloud

- Role-plays reading

Phonological Awareness: The child will demonstrate the ability to work with rhymes, words, syllables, onsets and rimes.

- Begins to hear, identify and make oral rhymes (e.g., "The pig has a wig")

- Shows increasing ability to hear, identify and work with syllables in spoken words (e.g., "I can clap the parts of my name: An-drew")

Phonemic Awareness: The child will demonstrate the ability to hear, identify and manipulate individual sounds in spoken words.

- Shows increasing ability to discriminate, identify and work with individual phonemes in spoken words (e.g., "The first sound in sun is /s/")

- Recognizes which words in a set of words begin with the same sound (e.g., "Bell, bike and boy all have /b/ at the beginning")

Phonics (Letter Knowledge and Early Word Recognition): The child will demonstrate the ability to apply sound-symbol relationships.

- Recognizes own name in print
- Demonstrates awareness or knowledge of letters of the English language, especially letters from own name
- Begins to recognize the sound association of some letters.

Vocabulary: The child will develop and expand knowledge of words and word meanings to increase vocabulary.

- Shows a steady increase in listening and speaking vocabulary
- Understands and follows oral directions (e.g., use of position words: under, above, through)
- Links new learning experiences and vocabulary to what is already known about a topic

Comprehension: The child will associate meaning and understanding with reading.

- Uses prereading skills and strategies (e.g., connecting prior knowledge to text, making predictions about text and using picture clues)
- Demonstrates progress in abilities to retell and dictate stories from books and experiences.
- Remembers and articulates some sequences of events
- Tells what is happening in a picture

Some excerpts from other areas:

Life Science

The child will observe and investigate plants and animals.

- Develops an awareness of what various plants and animals need for growth
- Demonstrates a beginning awareness of the changes that plants and animals go through during their life (e.g., seed to plant, egg to chicken)
- Demonstrates an interest and respect for the plant and animal life around them

Economics

The child will explore various careers.

- Develops growing awareness of jobs and what is required to perform them
- Identifies various school and community personnel
- Develops an awareness of money being needed to purchase things

Social and Personal Skills

The child will participate in activities to develop the skills necessary for working and interacting with others.

- Plays, works and interacts easily with one or more children and/or adults
- Begins to develop relationships with others
- Shows respect for others and their property
- Develops increasing abilities to give and take in interactions, to take turns in games or using materials, to interact without being overly submissive or directive

The child will develop the skills necessary for participating in a variety of settings.

- States his or her full name, age and name of parent or guardian.
- Shows ability to adjust to new situations.

MARYLAND

Mathematics

Algebra, Patterns and/or Functions: Students will algebraically represent, model, analyze or solve mathematical or real-world problems involving patterns or functional relationships.

- Match patterns kinesthetically (e.g., clap/snap/clap ...)

- Represent simple repeating patterns using no more than two different objects and different actions in the core of the pattern

- Explore relationships by comparing groups of no more than five objects to determine more or less

Geometry: Students will apply the properties of one-, two- or three-dimensional geometric figures to describe reason, or solve problems about shape, size, position or motion of objects.

- Sort objects by one attribute, such as shape, color, size, weight or length

- Name the attribute of plane figures such as shape, color, size

- Identify triangles, circles, squares and solid figures in the environment

Measurement: Students will identify attributes of measurements or apply a variety of techniques, formulas, tools or technology for determining measurements.

- Demonstrate an understanding of comparative attributes such as bigger, smaller, longer, shorter, lighter, heavier, shorter, taller, hotter, colder

- Measure the length of objects

- Explore the weight of objects using a two-pan balance

Statistics: Students will collect, organize, display, analyze or interpret data to make decisions or predictions.

- Explore data by answering a yes/no question

- Display data on real graphs and picture graphs

- Talk about data on graphs to answer a question such as, "Which category has the most?"

Number Relationships or Computations: Students will describe, represent or apply numbers or their relationships or will estimate or compute using mental strategies, paper/pencil or technology

- Show an understanding of quantity

- Use concrete materials to build sets 0 to 5; count to 10

- Use ordinal words to indicate position such as first, next and last

Processes of Mathematics: Students demonstrate the process of mathematics by making connections and applying reasoning to solve and to communicate their findings.

- Identify the question in the problem

- Decide if enough information is present to solve the problem

- Explain mathematical ideas orally

- Identify mathematics within other disciplines

Some excerpts from other areas:

Visual Arts

Aesthetic Education: Students will demonstrate the ability to perceive, interpret and respond to ideas, experiences and the environment through art.

- Identify colors, lines and shapes that are found in the environment
- Identify the subject matter of various works or art
- Use color, line and shape to make artworks

Historical, Cultural and Social Context: Students will demonstrate an understanding of visual arts as a basic aspect of history and human experience.

- Identify and sort artwork by theme
- Use selected works of art as inspiration to express ideas visually and verbally
- Use a variety of visual art processes to express ideas

Physical Development

Motor Learning Principles: Students will demonstrate the ability to use motor skill principles to learn and develop proficiency through frequent practice opportunities in which skills are repeatedly performed correctly in a variety of situations.

- Experience a variety of age-appropriate activities that include walking, hopping, jumping, etc.
- Use verbal and visual cues to improve personal performance

Personal and Social Development

Emotional Self-Regulations: Students will demonstrate effective emotional functioning in group settings as individuals.

- Attempts new play and learning experiences independently
- Relates his needs, wants and feelings to others
- Generates and follows classroom rules

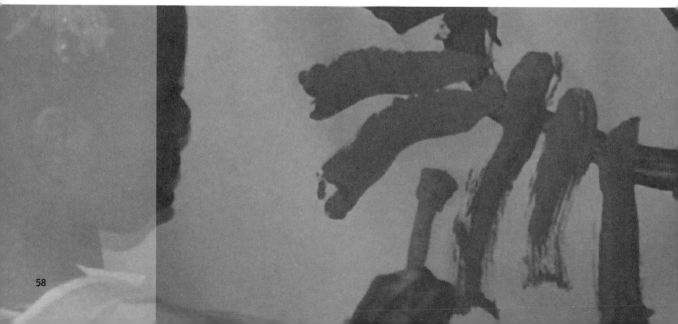

Teaching Literacy and Numeracy

Within the pre-K environment, principals expect teachers to incorporate practices that stimulate early literacy. The following examples for teachers were published by the National Association for the Education of Young Children in its guide, *Learning To Read and Write: Developmentally Appropriate Practices for Young Children.*

- Stimulating growth in children's vocabulary: Introducing new words in relation to familiar concepts and making sure that children have plenty of chances to hear and use new words informally

- Creating print-rich classroom environments by labeling items with children's names, names of colors and familiar words

- Helping children learn to handle and look at books, holding them to see the pictures and noticing the words on the page

- Reading aloud to children in the classroom on a regular basis

- Helping children hear the sounds that make up words, changing beginnings and endings to create rhyming words and other similar sounds

- Introducing letters of the alphabet so that children understand the relationship between letters and sounds.

In the same way, early numeracy is introduced through experiences in the classroom by counting, measuring and experiencing differences in size and shape, and understanding mathematical ideas such as "more" and "less." As examples, teachers can begin by:

- Scooping and measuring beans or other items to understand how much different measuring cups or scoops can hold

- Measuring how tall children are or how long an object is to get an idea of relative size and shape

- Picking up objects of different sizes to understand how heavy they are

- Having children count as they make objects and begin to learn more and less as they manipulate them

Questions for Further Reflection

Effective principals ensure quality curriculum and instructional practices that foster young children's learning and development.

Foster young children's eagerness to learn.

How do we stimulate children's curiosity throughout the school? How do we encourage all children to make sense of their experiences and environment? How can I encourage adults in the school community to be engaged in continuous learning?

Develop early literacy and early numeracy skills to provide a foundation for later learning.

How do I communicate the importance of early learning in literacy and numeracy? How can teachers build a true continuum of learning that leads to reading? How can we promote and celebrate literacy throughout the school and in the community? How can we incorporate basic math concepts and skills into the pre-K environment? How well do programs connect learning experiences across disciplines and help build skills in subjects beyond math and language arts?

Provide ongoing professional development for the school community to build an eagerness to learn.

How do we, as a professional learning community, honor and strengthen our own desire to learn? How can we encourage continuous learning for children, staff, families and community members? How can we make learning something students enjoy in our school?

Standard Four Strategies

Use the Questions for Further Reflection to help you think about and rate the degree to which each Standard Four strategy is evident in your school or in your practice as a school leader.

1 Not evident in my school/practice

2 Somewhat or occasionally evident in school/practice

3 Consistently evident in school/practice

4 Consistently evident, with practices that elaborate upon or exceed expectation

Self-Assessment: Beginning of the Year	1	2	3	4
Foster young children's eagerness to learn.				
Develop early literacy and early numeracy skills to provide a foundation for later learning.				
Provide ongoing professional development for the school community to build an eagerness to learn.				

Notes/Action Steps: Beginning of the Year

Self-Assessment: Middle of the Year	1	2	3	4
Foster young children's eagerness to learn.				
Develop early literacy and early numeracy skills to provide a foundation for later learning.				
Provide ongoing professional development for the school community to build an eagerness to learn.				

Notes/Action Steps: Middle of the Year

Self-Assessment: End of the Year	1	2	3	4
Foster young children's eagerness to learn.				
Develop early literacy and early numeracy skills to provide a foundation for later learning.				
Provide ongoing professional development for the school community to build an eagerness to learn.				

Notes/Action Steps: End of the Year

61

For More Information

On the Web

Gesell Institute of Human Development (www.gesellinstitute.org) is dedicated to understanding how children grow and learn. The institute has developed a standard of norms that illustrate a sequential and predictable pattern of growth and development.

International Reading Association (www.reading.org) and the **National Association for the Education of Young Children** (www.naeyc.org) have published a joint position statement, *Learning To Read and Write: Developmentally Appropriate Practices for Young Children.*

National Council of Teachers of Mathematics (www.nctm.org) and the **National Association for the Education of Young Children** (www.naeyc.org) have published a joint position statement, *Early Childhood Mathematics: Promoting Good Beginnings.*

From the Research

Collay, Michelle, Diane Dunlap, Walter Enloe and George W. Gagnon, Jr. *Learning Circles: Creating Conditions for Professional Development.* Thousand Oaks, CA, Corwin Press, 1998.

Katz, L. G. "Educating Young Children." *Streamlined Seminar*, Vol. 21, No. 3, National Association of Elementary School Principals, Spring 2003.

Neuman, S. B., C. Copple and S. Bredekamp. *Learning To Read and Write: Developmentally Appropriate Practices for Young Children.* Washington, DC: National Association for the Education of Young Children, 2002.

Sornson, Bob, Ed. *Preventing Early Learning Failure.* Alexandria, VA: Association for Supervision and Curriculum Development, 2001.

Standard Five: Use Multiple Assessments To Strengthen Learning

Effective principals use multiple assessments to create experiences that strengthen student learning.

Assessing young children's learning—what they know and are able to do—is challenging. Standards-based education, and the accompanying assessments to ensure students are learning the standards, is taking hold in elementary and upper grades. Some state and local policymakers are recommending similar guidelines for pre-K classes as well.

Such guidelines can clarify expectations for school readiness. When they are extended to standardized testing, however, principals need to provide a leading voice in explaining that skilled teachers are the best judges of pre-K growth and performance. Young children's performance can be inconsistent. They may be able to perform a task one day but not the next. Attempting to measure pre-K learning on a standardized exam for accountability purposes is not likely to yield useful information.

However, appropriate assessments used in classrooms by teachers and principals are a key ingredient in building high-quality pre-K programs and forging paths to students' intellectual growth. Assessments built around teachers' observations and analysis of students' work can help create a true continuum of early childhood learning that allows children to steadily build new skills and knowledge from pre-K through the start of fourth grade.

When principals with a strong understanding of early childhood development help teachers assess and make sense of children's learning on an ongoing basis, we see principals who:

- Support teachers in using observation, records and portfolios of student work to guide students' growth

- Use data from assessments to identify learning barriers, design strategies to overcome them, plan new learning experiences and initiate discussions across grade levels

- Share information about program effectiveness between school systems and other providers

- Educate parents and report to them about their children's development and individual progress

Support teachers in using observation, anecdotal records and portfolios of student work to guide students' growth.

Authentic assessment, which reflects a child's performance during typical activities in the classroom, leads to sound educational decisions focused on an individual child's performance. Assessment practices in developmentally appropriate classrooms include collections of children's work in portfolios, audio recordings of their reading, teacher observation and summaries of children's progress.

Principals know that assessment of young children's learning is not a snapshot of a single event but an ongoing process. They expect teachers to write regularly about every child's classroom learning and interactions. Documenting changes in behavior and knowledge over time creates a living record of children's development.

Portfolios—examples of children's work—supplement teachers' records. For pre-K children, portfolios may include drawings, paintings and samples of projects. Often, teachers will talk with children about their work and write what the child says, including the child's natural language in describing their work and learning as part of the portfolio.

Principals support teachers in this work by asking them to share their records and student portfolios with other teachers in the learning community and expressing questions or concerns. They ensure that teachers have adequate time to create and update assessments.

Use data from assessments to identify learning barriers, design strategies to overcome them, plan new learning experiences and initiate discussions across grade levels.

Principals help teachers who document children's learning use that information to strengthen classroom practice. Principals convene teachers across the early childhood continuum to:

- Examine samples of students' work to understand individual development
- Look for patterns of strengths and weaknesses across the group to determine the effect of current practice
- Share practices that worked in similar situations
- Strengthen teaching across the continuum of learning from pre-K through the start of fourth grade

In these sessions, principals use their instructional leadership to raise issues that extend teachers' thinking, suggest additional resources and curriculum materials, and help teachers determine how to implement changes in their classrooms.

Principals make time to visit classrooms to see how assessments and the information gleaned from them are being implemented.

Share information about program effectiveness between school systems and other providers.

Even principals with pre-K programs in their buildings can open new lines of communication with community pre-K providers to strengthen students' skills when they enter kindergarten or first grade. Many school districts assess children's skill levels when they enter kindergarten, and principals can notify or convene pre-K providers to share the results of these assessments, so they can tailor future programs accordingly.

Some pre-K providers in the community may also have gathered important information about children through their daily observations and ongoing assessments. Head Start regulations require programs to connect with a child's next school to facilitate a smooth transition. Head Start officials report that, traditionally, many principals have not shown much interest in sharing information and data. Where information on pre-K students' progress exists, principals should make sure it is shared and used.

A collaborative process strengthens the connection between public schools and other providers, offers valuable direction for strengthening student learning and begins to develop a professional community including all those in a community who work with pre-K children.

The Work Sampling System

Many pre-K programs use the Work Sampling System to document children's skills, knowledge, behavior and accomplishments across curriculum areas over time to enhance teaching and learning. Because it establishes categories for observing and documenting student work, the WSS more readily allows teachers to track students in specific areas over time. The WSS can be used to document students' progress from pre-K through third grade, allowing teachers to track individual students' progress and understand the impact of pre-K programs on later learning.

The WSS includes three components:

• Developmental Guidelines and Checklists assist teachers in observing and documenting individual children's growth and progress. Each checklist (structured for children from pre-K through fifth grade) covers seven domains: personal and social development; language and literacy; mathematical thinking; scientific thinking; social studies; the arts and physical development.

• Portfolios are planned collections of children's work that show their efforts, progress and achievements. They provide a clear picture of each child's work throughout the year.

• Summary Reports, completed three times a year, use teacher observations and records specified by the WSS. Summary reports translate information into a document that is easy for parents, teachers and administrators to discuss. Summary reports are designed to replace report cards. They include performance and progress ratings in each domain listed above and teachers' reflections and comments about a child's development based on evidence accumulated in the checklists and portfolios.

FOCUS ON PRACTICE

Spreading the Word on What Students Need

Columbia Elementary School, Rochester, Indiana

At Columbia Elementary School Principal Cheryl Downs starts working on preschoolers' education months before their first day of kindergarten.

"There are developmental windows that are closing before we can get our hands on our students," she said. "If we can get literacy awareness started before they get here, we have a better chance for a successful, happy learner."

For five years, Downs has informed area pre-K, Head Start and child care providers about the strengths and weaknesses revealed in spring assessments of the next fall's incoming kindergarten classes. The information on visual and motor skills, speech needs, vocabulary development, letter and sound awareness and language concepts is also used in the pre-K class the school operates.

After reviewing the results, Downs may urge local programs to beef up skills like the difference between being over, on or under an object or exposure to concepts like quantity or time. The information about the strengths and weaknesses of a new crop of kindergarteners means teachers have a better idea of individual and group learning needs right away.

Analysis of brain research led the small-town pre-K-2 school to seek new ways to influence what happens with students before they start kindergarten. Adopting the slogan "Frontload for Success," Downs said sharing data from the spring assessments with parents and pre-K providers has been a big hit.

"They're happy to get it, and in fact, the more specific we are, the better they like it," the 10th-year principal said.

Sharing the wisdom gained from assessments drives teachers' work inside the school, too. Teachers study student work and test results to guide their work in removing barriers to learning. The staff is familiar with the process of formulating theories, restructuring teaching methods, testing the results and fine-tuning.

"Our collective kindergarten data for five years indicates we are having more success and fewer failures in the primary grades. Our community is happy with that," Downs said. "We have seen results, and that has helped us raise our expectations."

Educate parents and report to them about their children's development and individual progress.

Children's and their parents' participation in both goal-setting and evaluation is integral to a high-quality assessment process.

As partners in their children's learning, parents and other family members benefit from face-to-face talks with teachers to learn about their children's development. Parents may need help learning about typical development at specific ages to understand their own child's development and progress. Conversations between parents and teachers also set the stage for families to be involved in supporting their children's learning beyond pre-K.

Principals support these conversations by providing teachers with the flexibility to schedule conferences at times and locations convenient for parents. Principals observe or participate in conferences to ensure a positive tone and effective communication.

Principals also communicate to parents that the school does not provide traditional "report cards" to pre-K students. And the principal and teacher are available to answer parents' questions about standardized testing and the appropriate role of assessment in pre-K programs.

PRINCIPALS' VOICES

"Delaware has a state tracking system and statewide identification number for all students. If a child enters the school in March, we have the history of that child and can go back and see where the child is. That system has been very helpful."

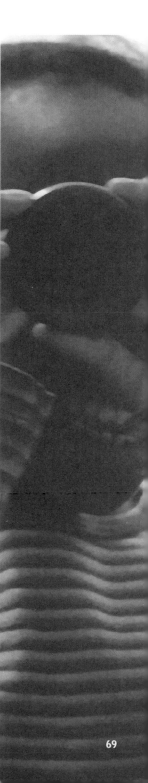

FOCUS ON PRACTICE

Weaving Play Time Together With Accountability

Morris Early Childhood Center, Lincoln, Delaware

Creating the best possible environment for young children to learn has led Delaware princi-pal Beth Carlson right into the force of the state's drive for higher academic standards and expanded testing. Bit by bit, she says she feels like she's succeeding at making school engaging while still delivering quality academics.

Last year, Carlson helped launch an effort to have Delaware lawmakers reconsider statewide testing for kindergarten and first-grade students.

After presentations from Carlson and others that the state's testing system failed to pro-vide meaningful results, lawmakers eliminated testing before second grade.

"The state was using the most developmentally appropriate tool, but it wasn't providing us with useful information," Carlson said. "We said, 'Let's reallocate those resources spent on state testing and instead give our kids as much instruction as possible.'"

At the Morris Early Childhood Center, issues that involve children ages six and under are all that matter. The pre-K-1 program serves about 700 children from across the district and includes four pre-K classes, 19 sections of kindergarten and 16 first grades.

While state testing in kindergarten and first grade no longer looms, Carlson said that the pressure of state standards remains. For example, students in her district are expected to recognize 57 sight words by the end of kindergarten. The third-year principal said she has to take a stand when teachers ask whether they should skip time painting at easels in favor of drills with flashcards.

"A big question is how we keep the sense of play and adventure in an era of higher accountability," Carlson said. "My answer is that we need to keep that playfulness and love of learning. We have to keep singing songs and working with Play-Doh or visiting the pumpkin patch, but within all of that, we have to make everything very purposeful and meaningful."

Questions for Further Reflection

Effective principals use multiple assessments to create experiences that strengthen student learning.

Support teachers in using observation, anecdotal records and portfolios of student work to guide students' growth.

How can I strengthen my own skills in observing and documenting students' growth? How can I support teachers in using multiple measures to assess students?

Use data from assessments to identify learning barriers, design strategies to overcome them, plan new learning experiences and initiate discussions across grade levels.

How can assessments be part of a process that brings a continuum of learning to life by easing transitions from pre-K through the start of fourth grade? How can we build a learning community among teachers to strengthen practice? How can we track students' strengths and weaknesses across age and grade levels? What additional experiences and supports do our children need to be successful?

Share information about program effectiveness between school systems and other providers.

What pre-K or child care programs do children in our community attend? How can I strengthen connections between pre-K and child care programs in the community and our school? What do results of kindergarten entry screenings or other tests tell us about children's learning needs?

Educate parents and report to them about their children's cognitive development and individual progress.

What can we learn from parents about their children's development and learning? How can we use parent-teacher collaboration to strengthen students' learning? How can I strengthen communication between parents and teachers?

Standard Five Strategies

Use the Questions for Further Reflection to help you think about and rate the degree to which each Standard Five strategy is evident in your school or in your practice as a school leader.

1 Not evident in my school/practice

2 Somewhat or occasionally evident in school/practice

3 Consistently evident in school/practice

4 Consistently evident, with practices that elaborate upon or exceed expectation

Self-Assessment: Beginning of the Year	1	2	3	4
Support teachers in using observation, records and portfolios of student work to guide students' growth.				
Use data from assessments to identify learning barriers, design strategies to overcome them, plan new learning experiences and initiate discussions across grade levels.				
Educate parents and report to them about their children's development and individual progress.				

Notes/Action Steps: Beginning of the Year

Self-Assessment: Middle of the Year	1	2	3	4
Support teachers in using observation, records and portfolios of student work to guide students' growth.				
Use data from assessments to identify learning barriers, design strategies to overcome them, plan new learning experiences and initiate discussions across grade levels.				
Educate parents and report to them about their children's development and individual progress.				

Notes/Action Steps: Middle of the Year

Self-Assessment: End of the Year	1	2	3	4
Support teachers in using observation, records and portfolios of student work to guide students' growth.				
Use data from assessments to identify learning barriers, design strategies to overcome them, plan new learning experiences and initiate discussions across grade levels.				
Educate parents and report to them about their children's development and individual progress.				

Notes/Action Steps: End of the Year

For More Information

On the Web

ERIC Digest (www.ericdigests.org) includes a short article on *Performance Assessment in Early Childhood Education: The Work Sampling System.*

High/Scope Educational Research Foundation (www.highscope.org/Assessment/homepage.htm) publishes documents and instruments for assessment in preschool and early elementary school programs.

National Institute for Early Education Research (www.nieer.org) has a wealth of resources, including the policy brief *Preschool Assessment: A Guide to Developing a Balanced Approach.*

From the Research

Grace, C. and E. F. Shores. *The Portfolio Book: A Step-by-Step Guide for Teachers.* Beltsville, MD: Gryphon House, 1998.

McAfee, Oralie, Deborah J. Leong, and Elena Bodrova. *Basics of Assessment: A Primer for Early Childhood Educators.* Washington, DC, National Association for the Education of Young Children, 2004.

Meisels, Samuel J. "Using Work Sampling in Authentic Assessments." *Educational Leadership*, Vol. 54, No. 4, December 1996/January 1997.

Standard Six: Advocate for High-Quality, Universal Early Childhood Education

Effective principals advocate for universal opportunity for children to attend high-quality early childhood education programs.

The movement to make pre-K programs available to all parents is growing nationally. Principals who know the needs of young children in their communities can play a pivotal role in making the case for expanding high-quality pre-K programs.

A recent poll conducted by Fight Crime: Invest in Kids found that kindergarten teachers believe that children who had not had access to pre-K programs were substantially less prepared to succeed in school than those who had attended pre-kindergarten. Nine of 10 teachers agreed that "substantially more" children would succeed in school if all families had access to high-quality pre-K programs.

Leading business organizations and economists also lend their influence to the importance of pre-K and kindergarten programs. The Business Roundtable and the Committee for Economic Development issued policy statements in 2004 supporting expanded opportunities for pre-K programs. Nobel Prize-winning economist James Heckman has concluded:

"We cannot afford to postpone investing in children until they become adults, nor can we wait until they reach school age—a time when it may be too late to intervene. Learning is a dynamic process and is most effective when it begins at a young age and continues through adulthood."

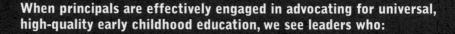

When principals are effectively engaged in advocating for universal, high-quality early childhood education, we see leaders who:

- Use the trusted voice of the principal to advocate for the needs of young children in their communities

- Become familiar with early childhood funding streams and policy issues

- Keep the public and policymakers focused on the need for full-day kindergarten for all children and the importance of high-quality pre-K in a continuum of learning that helps children and schools succeed

Use the trusted voice of the principal to advocate for the needs of young children in their communities.

Schools focused on building a strong continuum across the community to better educate young children form strong connections to families, community organizations and individuals and organizations serving children and families. This web of connections expands the principal's role: Principals become community leaders, not just school leaders. They become representatives for school systems and the importance of children starting school ready to learn. They are advocates for young children's needs, not just for education and schools.

As leaders in education, principals are well-positioned to speak publicly on behalf of children, whether or not the children are enrolled in elementary school. They can carry the message about the need for high-quality pre-K programs as a central focus of their advocacy.

Principals sometimes think of advocacy only in political terms—making a speech or carrying a petition on behalf of specific legislation or candidate. Advocacy also carries a broader meaning: Speaking out on behalf of a cause or a concern.

Principals can expect professional organizations, such as NAESP and its affiliates, to take a leadership role in political advocacy. But principals must also make their individual concerns known. At the local level, principals can promote the benefits of high-quality pre-K programs with staff members, parents and others in the school community; with principals and other leaders in the school district; with colleagues in groups such as local early childhood coordinating councils and with individuals and groups in the larger community, including elected representatives and policymakers.

PRINCIPALS' VOICES

"We should not just be engaged in getting funding, but in larger issues such as ensuring high-quality programs in all settings."

Principals who speak out about the importance of high-quality early childhood education in their communities take that position based on evidence that children benefit: They are more likely to succeed in school; they develop stronger, more positive relationships with adults and peers alike; and they are likely to have long-term educational, social and financial gains. Principals are strongest and most credible as advocates when they combine their knowledge of research and advocacy from other groups with examples from their own experience, such as:

- Children who made gains in learning and behavior during their pre-K experience
- Children who succeeded in kindergarten and beyond as a result of their experience
- Declines in behavior problems in the school as a result of succeeding in pre-K

These examples can be as simple as a story about an individual child and his or her family. They are even more effective when they include some data such as, "Of the 35 children who were in our pre-K program in 2001-02, not one had to be held back in first grade."

Principals should not underestimate the value of keeping local, state and federal officials abreast of children's needs and school successes, particularly in programs like kindergarten, pre-K and Head Start. Government leaders are more likely to back programs when they know of concrete examples of ways they are achieving their goals and making a positive difference in communities. Principals should also recognize the influence they carry when they speak with other community and government leaders.

Become familiar with early childhood funding streams and policy issues.

In most school districts, schools that provide pre-K programs use a variety of federal, state and local funding. At the federal level, these programs are often tied to specific eligibility criteria, such as income levels for Head Start programs and a diagnosed disability for special education.

Many school districts use a portion of their federal Title I funds for pre-K programs or allow principals to allocate Title I funds at the site level for that purpose. Other federal grant programs that can also support pre-K programs include Even Start and Early Reading First.

State funding for pre-K and kindergarten programs vary, with some states providing no funding at all. Two states—Georgia and Oklahoma—provide opportunities for pre-K and kindergarten programs for all children whose parents choose to enroll them, but significant campaigns to expand opportunities are under way in several states. Whether or not programs are housed in schools, most states provide some funding for pre-K and kindergarten programs for low-income students and several are expanding programs to serve more young people.

FROM THE FIELD

"Principals can be messengers of the importance of early childhood education and what parents and other community members can do to make sure early education programs exist and are of quality."

Julie Bosland, National League of Cities

Keep the public and policymakers focused on the need for full-day kindergarten for all children and the importance of high-quality pre-K in a continuum of learning that helps children and schools succeed.

PRINCIPALS' VOICES

"Kindergarten is what first grade used to be —in half the time."

In some states, readiness for schools still centers on providing kindergarten programs for all children. According to the Foundation for Child Development, "Kindergarten suffers from the middle-child syndrome, caught between early childhood education and compulsory public education, even though it shares features with both education levels." Most states do not support full-day kindergarten for all students, despite research that has shown that it is advantageous.

States and communities differ on the preferred location for pre-K programs and which agencies should operate them. In Oklahoma, all public pre-K programs are part of the public schools. Georgia, meanwhile, provides funds for programs in school- and community-based settings. This is often a matter of community preference, with a commitment to allowing parents to enroll their children in settings that reflect the values and cultures of home and family. The choice of location may also reflect a need for space, which is not readily available in crowded urban communities.

Principals who promote the value of early childhood education use their position and credibility to validate the importance of high-quality pre-K programs, no matter who operates them, and to ensure that all education programs in the community are designed and coordinated to prepare all young children for success in school and in life.

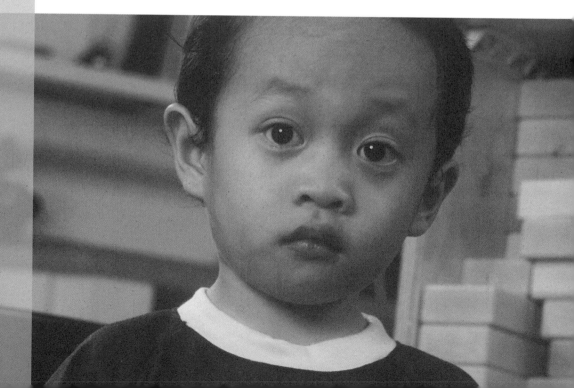

FOCUS ON PRACTICE

Pushing for Pre-K in Every Arena

Clays Mill Elementary, Scottsburg, Virginia

Sherman LaPrade has found many avenues to work toward quality pre-K programs during his 12 years as a principal in Virginia. He's helped elevate the issue as a priority in the state elementary principals association, he advocates for the issue in his district, and he's taken a keen interest in the pre-K programs in schools where he's worked.

"I'd love to see the day when [pre-K] programs are mandatory in every elementary school," he said. "For now, we have to keep pushing through the space and financial issues and show it's important to ensure that kids get early help in areas where they may already be falling behind."

That means that, while not every preschooler has access to pre-K in a public school, LaPrade believes that principals should be reaching out to pre-K programs in their neighborhood and community.

While he was principal at Bacon District Elementary School in Charlotte County, Virginia, LaPrade worked to connect the school's Head Start program, pre-K and kindergarten so that the three-year-olds who came to the school would be working toward consistent goals from the beginning.

As a board member for the Virginia Association of Elementary School Principals, LaPrade has worked to expand interest and increase funding for quality early childhood programs.

"I think every principal would love to have pre-K and a full-day kindergarten, and lots of people will say they are in favor of early childhood programs. But building capacity and funding is a problem," he said. LaPrade added that a pre-K program would be a big help at Clays Mill Elementary, the 310-student K-6 school where he is now principal.

Beyond advocacy and building quality in the programs that now exist, LaPrade encourages principals to open lines of communication with private child care providers and pre-K programs at churches and other venues to boost awareness of kindergarten expectations. "We need to improve children's readiness for school any way we can," he said.

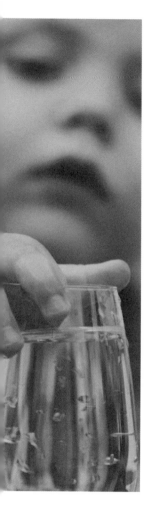

Take Action

Principals have many opportunities to be advocates for the needs of young children. To promote pre-K programs in your community, you can:

- Take a leadership role in a coalition of organizations that work with young children to promote quality programs and readiness for kindergarten or first grade

- Convene a group of principals to study quality pre-K programs and discuss ways to build support in the community, region or state

- Talk to your local school board about the relationship between pre-K programs and later success. Emphasize the importance of improved salary, better pay structures and quality training for early childhood teachers

- Invite local leaders and state and federal legislators to your school to see how young children are learning and describe your efforts or needs to improve early learning

- Get to know your state's two U.S. senators and your area's U.S. representative and give them information about early childhood education in your area. Be in touch with them on a regular basis, either on your own or as an NAESP Key Contact

- Write a letter to the editor of your local newspaper to share findings from research about the costs and benefits of quality early childhood programs

- Advocate for federal policies that would fully fund Head Start and increase resources and attention focused on early childhood programs and improving school readiness

FOCUS ON PRACTICE

Creating New Opportunities Through Community Alliances

Oakland Heights Elementary School, Meridian, Mississippi

According to Principal Kim Benton, pre-K revived Oakland Heights Elementary School over the past nine years.

"We've gone from being just any school in an ordinary part of town to having a strong reputation and a success rate that's right there with our top-scoring elementary school. It all goes back to our preschool and the relationships we built from there," Benton said.

Connections started with organizations like Meridian Community College, which supplied volunteers, and the Barksdale Reading Institute, which helped create a resource center for parents. The pre-K-5 school took a dramatic step forward this year by opening a pre-K classroom in a nearby housing project.

Benton supervises the 16-student program at the housing project in addition to her duties at the 600-student elementary school. A grant pays for the teacher at the housing project classroom, who is on the staff of Oakland Heights. The district provides materials, and the local housing authority offers space.

A classroom off campus was a logical step for a program built around finding ways to increase participation and achievement.

"Nobody minds investing in things when they see results, and we've focused on making our preschool something the community was involved in," Benton said. "I talk to everybody— Rotary, Lions, Civitans—we get local businesspeople in here to see what's happening, and we've found ways to work with every organization possible. They know about our results, too, which opens more doors."

Oakland Heights launched the district's first pre-K classroom after screenings showed its five-year-olds started kindergarten with the language skills of two- and three-year-olds. The enthusiasm that surrounded the pre-K's opening hasn't waned, the 10th-year principal said. Pre-K is now common in Meridian's schools.

"Everyone wants to be part of something that's working," Benton said. "This program is a symbol of commitment from an entire community to move forward."

Questions for Further Reflection

Effective principals advocate for universal opportunity for children to attend high-quality early childhood education programs.

Use the trusted voice of the principal to advocate for the needs of young children in their communities.

What do leaders in my community know about young children's development and learning? How can I use my position and understanding to raise community awareness and support? Who are other leaders who can be champions for quality pre-K programs in our community?

Become familiar with early childhood funding streams and policy issues.

What sources of funding do our school, district and state use to support pre-K programs? What other opportunities might be available to us? What are the chief policy issues facing pre-K and improving school readiness in this state and in Congress?

Keep the public and policymakers focused on the need for full-day kindergarten for all children and the importance of quality pre-K in a continuum of learning that helps children and schools succeed.

How can we make the best use of opportunities to expand pre-K programs? How can we build a coalition of educators and others to keep the community and elected officials apprised of children's needs when it comes to kindergarten and pre-K? What could leaders in our school and district do to raise the profile of this issue?

Standard Six Strategies

Use the Questions for Further Reflection to help you think about and rate the degree to which each Standard Six strategy is evident in your school or in your practice as a school leader.

1 Not evident in my school/practice

2 Somewhat or occasionally evident in school/practice

3 Consistently evident in school/practice

4 Consistently evident, with practices that elaborate upon or exceed expectation

Self-Assessment: Beginning of the Year	1	2	3	4
Use the trusted voice of the principal to advocate for the needs of young children in their communities.				
Become familiar with early childhood funding streams and policy issues.				
Keep the public and policymakers focused on the need for full-day kindergarten for all children and the importance of quality pre-K in a continuum of learning that helps children and schools succeed.				

Notes/Action Steps: Beginning of the Year

Self-Assessment: Beginning of the Year	1	2	3	4
Use the trusted voice of the principal to advocate for the needs of young children in their communities.				
Become familiar with early childhood funding streams and policy issues.				
Keep the public and policymakers focused on the need for full-day kindergarten for all children and the importance of quality pre-K in a continuum of learning that helps children and schools succeed.				

Notes/Action Steps: Beginning of the Year

Self-Assessment: Beginning of the Year	1	2	3	4
Use the trusted voice of the principal to advocate for the needs of young children in their communities.				
Become familiar with early childhood funding streams and policy issues.				
Keep the public and policymakers focused on the need for full-day kindergarten for all children and the importance of quality pre-K in a continuum of learning that helps children and schools succeed.				

Notes/Action Steps: Beginning of the Year

For More Information

On the Web

Fight Crime: Invest in Kids (www.fightcrime.org) has published a national poll of kindergarten teachers on the value of pre-K programs.

Committee for Economic Development (www.ced.org) features *The Productivity Argument for Investing in Young Children* by Nobel laureate James Heckman and *Preschool for All: Investing in a Productive and Just Society*, a statement from the research and policy committee.

Pre-K Now (www.preknow.org) includes detailed information for advocates for pre-K programs, including a primer on quality pre-K programs that is designed to serve as a detailed guide for the field.

National Institute for Early Education Research (wwww.nieer.org) produces an annual report, *The State of Preschool*, which charts individual states' commitment to preschool education, as well as other research-based resources regarding early childhood education.

Ounce of Prevention Fund (www.ounceofprevention.org) provides essential knowledge and skills to practitioners, policymakers and parents to help in the healthy development of children and their families. It also offers Nobel Laureate James Heckman's "Invest in the Very Young," which clearly points out the high returns from an early investment in education.

From the Research

Lynch, Robert G. *Exceptional Returns: Economic, Fiscal and Social Benefits of Investment in Early Childhood Development.* Washington, DC: Economic Policy Institute, 2004.

Key Terms and Definitions

These definitions have been culled from NAESP's writings, as well as from the research and writing of its partners.

Academic Goals refer to state standards that define what children should know or be able to do at certain grade levels. The term is usually associated with formal methods of instruction. Tasks associated with academic goals involve memorizing lists or symbols, responding to questions that have correct answers and practicing routine tasks that can be assessed as right or wrong.

Active Learning encourages children to be mentally and physically active, to manipulate real objects and to learn through hands-on experience. Active learning also provides opportunities for children to explore, reflect, interact and communicate with other children and adults.

Age Appropriate describes practices and environments that reflect what is known about child development and learning in relation to human development over an age span. Human development includes children's gross motor, fine motor, linguistic, cognitive, social and emotional skills. An understanding of human development guides planning for the learning environment and activities in early childhood. In order for practices and environments to be developmentally appropriate, they must be both age appropriate and individually appropriate.

Authentic Assessment engages students in tasks closely connected to real-life situations to determine their mastery of particular skills. Authentic assessment moves away from traditional academic assessments or standardized testing. In pre-K programs, authentic assessment helps build an understanding of a student's physical, social, emotional, intellectual and general knowledge development.

Child Care Programs encompass all types of community early education programs and child care centers. Child care programs are often licensed by the county or state to provide care for children while their parents are working or at school. These may be either for profit or nonprofit and can be part of a community center, a church or a free-standing child care center.

Cognitive Development during early childhood, which includes building skills such as pre-reading, language, vocabulary and numeracy, begins from the moment a child is born. Developmental scientists have found a strong connection between the development a child undergoes early in life and the level of success that the child will experience later in life. For example, infants who are better at distinguishing the building blocks of speech at six months are better at other more complex language skills at two and three years of age and better at acquiring the skills for learning to read at four and five years of age. Not surprisingly, a child's knowledge of the alphabet in kindergarten is one of the most significant predictors of what that child's tenth grade reading ability will be.

Continuum of Early Childhood Education is the span of learning from conception to age eight. This period includes the integration of three distinct periods, birth to age three, followed by preschool for three- and four-year-old, followed by the first three to four years of elementary school. Preschool is the period from birth to school entry at age five.

Developmentally Appropriate describes practices and environments created to serve children at their individual stages of learning. Developmentally appropriate practices and environments address the social and physical needs of the children; create varied opportunities for learning; address knowledge, skills, attitude toward learning and feelings. These practices emphasize positive and supportive interaction between staff and children, among adults in the classroom and among children. Materials and learning activities should also be evaluated for their appropriateness. In order for practices and environments to be developmentally appropriate, they must be both age appropriate and individually appropriate and ensure that learning expectations are meaningful, relevant and respectful—based on knowledge of the social and cultural contexts in which children live.

Dispositions for Learning is a phrase often used in early childhood materials. In this guide, it has been reworded as a child's attitude toward learning or eagerness to learn. Dispositions for learning explains habits of mind or tendencies in responding to new information or learning experiences. The dispositions that children need to acquire or to strengthen—curiosity, creativity, cooperation, friendliness—are primarily learned from being around people who exhibit them and not from formal instruction.

Early Childhood describes the period of a child's life between birth and 8 years of age. This time period equates roughly with the first two stages of cognitive development as first defined by Jean Piaget.

Early Childhood Education refers to structured educational opportunities for children within the continuum of early childhood education, a period that is crucial to a child's long-term development.

Early Emotional Skills help children accurately identify, label and manage their feelings, thus develop coping strategies. This includes forming attention, planning and sequencing skills that contribute to both their behavioral and intellectual outcomes.

Early Intervention refers to the capacity to provide comprehensive, coordinated services for young children with special learning and developmental needs and their families. Early interventions that respond to developmental difficulties reduce the need for retention or remediation and can significantly affect school readiness and later learning.

Early Learning Experiences are distinct from the kind of teaching and instruction that is a hallmark of classrooms in later years. Early childhood advocates use the term to describe the kinds of play, investigation and other developmentally appropriate activities that set early childhood classrooms apart and help children develop new skills, knowledge, and an eagerness to learn

Early Literacy Skills include oral language, general cognitive and specific literacy skills, as well as comprehension and application of reading and writing concepts that children should develop before they begin formal literacy instruction. Developing early literacy skills does not mean teaching the alphabet. It means that students can discuss events in sequence, think symbolically and develop memory and attention skills.

Early Numeracy Skills should be developed within the continuum of learning to ensure later success in mathematics. Early numeracy refers to a child's capacity for quantitative thought and expression. Numeracy skills include the ability to match and name size, shape and patterns; count forward and backward; recognize numerals; identify more and less of a quantity.

Early Physical Skills refers to the development of both the fine and gross motor skills that allow children to physically interact with others and their surroundings.

Early Social Skills allow a child to have substantive and positive interactions and relationships with peers and adults. Early social skills include listening, questioning and coping.

Family Child Care providers care for children in their own homes. This type of care is usually less expensive; therefore lower income families often select this care option.

Fine Motor Skills involve the coordination of small muscles such as those in the hands. Fine motor skills can develop through activities such as cutting, pasting, coloring and buttoning.

Gross Motor Skills involve the muscle tone, muscle strength, quality of movement and range of movement. Gross motor skills require balance and coordination and can be developed through activities such as running, hopping, climbing and playing with balls.

Head Start and Early Head Start are comprehensive child development programs administered by the federal government that serve children from birth to age 5, pregnant women and their families. They have the overall goal of increasing the school readiness of young children in low-income families. Head Start, administered by Department of Health and Human Services, connects children and families with a range of comprehensive services to support optimal child development.

Home Visiting Services offer support to families in their homes. These programs are operated by a variety of organizations including local health clinics providing outreach and health education to parents or early intervention services for families of children with identified disabilities.

Individually Appropriate refers to practices and environments that attend to the strengths, interests and needs of each individual child, adapting for and responding to individual variation. Both disabilities and experiences are likely to affect individual development. In order for practices and environments to be developmentally appropriate, they must be both age appropriate and individually appropriate.

Kindergarten is the set of structured educational opportunities that ensure readiness for first grade, most often based in schools.

Play is the business of childhood and is important to a child's development and learning. According to Piaget, it is through play that children construct a sense of order and meaning out of their environment. What may not look rigorous to some involves a lot of work. Play builds imagination, promotes social skills, advances physical development and helps children work through their emotions.

Pre-kindergarten is the set of structured educational opportunities that ensure readiness for kindergarten, sometimes provided in schools but often provided in other settings including Head Start, child care, family child care and more. It is the beginning point of the continuum of early childhood education.

Readiness refers to children as being prepared for what they will learn and do in school. More than basic knowledge of language and math, readiness must consider a child's health and physical development, emotional well-being, social competence, approaches to learning, communicative skills and general knowledge.

Social Competency refers to children's ability to interact with and find acceptance from adults and their peers during social interactions. The degree to which a child develops his or her early social skills determines his or her social competence.

A Call to Action

NAESP believes that all students should have the opportunity to be ready for school. If they are to bridge the existing gap between learning opportunities from birth to school entry and learning in K-12 education, then school leaders will require support, professional development and public commitment. Principals simply cannot do it alone.

Research demonstrates the long-term return of investment in early education. James J. Heckman, a Nobel laureate in economics, has confirmed the wisdom of increasing public investments in young children: "The real question is how to use available funds wisely. The evidence supports the policy prescription: Invest in the very young."

Here are eight policies for which principals can advocate at the federal, state and local levels to ensure that every child in the United States has an opportunity to be ready to start school:

1. Provide universal opportunity for children to attend high-quality early childhood education programs. Universal preschool education may be the best investment Americans can make in our children's education—and our nation's future. Regardless of ethnic background or socioeconomic status, children who have rich learning activities do better in school and in life. All states should provide free universal preschool programs, staffed with qualified, certified and well-paid early childhood teachers and specialists.

2. Fully fund Head Start to include all eligible children and maintain it as a federal government program. NAESP strongly recommends that Head Start be fully funded for all eligible children. With increases in inflation and poverty, only one-half of eligible children receive Head Start's services. NAESP recommends an appropriation of at least an additional $1 billion for the next fiscal year and additional amounts in the subsequent years to achieve full funding and service.

In addition, NAESP calls for Head Start's comprehensive and quality performance standards to be improved or at least maintained. Outcomes-focused strategies demand high-quality inputs to succeed. Parental involvement, dental care, immunizations, other health care, social development and pre-literacy and number skills are all essential to the success of Head Start's children. Any reauthorization must meet or exceed Head Start program performance standards that exist today.

Finally, NAESP recommends that Early Head Start be expanded. Given that the first few years of life are the foundation for future success, expanded funding of Early Head Start would ensure that more infants and toddlers benefit from high-quality comprehensive services.

3. Create transition programs that ensure close contact among Head Start programs, preschools, daycare programs and public schools. Learning is not purely a cognitive exercise. We know that children cannot learn when they are hungry, sick or too worried about their home situation to concentrate in school. State and local policies must focus on school readiness as a comprehensive concept, including early learning, literacy and numeracy, social and emotional development, nutrition, health and family support.

Ill-conceived programs often take fragmented, piecemeal approaches to the complex issues families face. We must take a comprehensive approach that directly involves families and communities in program design, implementation and evaluation of programs. And we must do more to support the effective transition of children from home to preschool, from preschool to kindergarten and from third to fourth grade.

4. Provide full-day kindergarten for all five-year-olds and after-school programs for children from kindergarten through middle school. An impressive amount of research backs up the concept of full-day kindergarten that supports five-year-olds academically, socially and emotionally. More than one-half the children who attend kindergarten do so in a full-day setting, and there has been an increased national trend toward providing full-day kindergarten for all students. However, doubling time in the classroom does not necessarily double program quality. Ensuring quality requires changing the academic model to take advantage of the additional time.

In addition, we must also commit to after-school programs that provide wrap-around services for children from kindergarten through middle school. We need to acknowledge that a day that ends at 3 p.m. is not a full day for working parents. Some schools have begun to define a full day as being the same length as the workdays of mothers and fathers. This is important: The Children's Defense Fund says that 65 percent of mothers with children under six are in the labor force. Just as some elementary schools currently benefit from the 21st Century Community Learning Centers program, which helps to support safe, healthy and academic environments for children in primary grades, so too would all schools benefit from improving the options for working families.

5. Ensure that early childhood programs meet the needs of the whole child. Simply having programs is not enough. Programs must be well-designed, developmentally appropriate and meet the social, physical, emotional and academic needs of young children. In addition, they must be staffed with well-educated, well-paid early childhood teachers and preschool specialists. All developmentally appropriate classrooms have one thing in common: The focus will be on the development of the whole child. Such programs will encourage the growth of children's self-esteem, their cultural identities, their independence and their individual strengths.

Furthermore, NAESP urges that care be taken not to push academics and testing on young children before they are ready. While the federal No Child Left Behind Act expands testing, NAESP urges caution with regard to preschool children.

6. Keep a teacher-student ratio of not more than 15-to-1 in early childhood programs, kindergarten and grades one through three. Reducing class size can increase educational effectiveness. When fewer children are in classrooms, teachers have more time to devote to each child. In addition, managing the group requires less teacher time. As a result, teachers can have longer conversations with each child and more time to observe each child's interests and activities. Teachers can develop lesson plans that respond to individual children's learning styles, strengths and weaknesses. Small class size and better staff-child ratios also offer health and safety benefits.

All states should set research-based standards that jointly address class size, adult-to-child ratios, teacher qualifications and teaching practices.

7. Provide professional growth programs for principals in all areas of early childhood instruction. For decades, there has been a division between K-12 education and children's programs from birth to school entry, particularly formal preschool education. Too many educators seem to believe that authentic education does not begin until elementary school, and some regard preschool education as babysitting that has little relevance to learning. Changing this mindset will not happen overnight.

Federal, state and local education agencies should promote efforts to build the capacity of principals to ensure an understanding of the important linkages between preschool and K-12 education and provide resources and flexibility to help them connect these integral elements of learning.

Principals also need support in recruiting qualified teachers, who are a critical component of all quality early childhood programs. Education and training levels of teachers are the strongest predictors of quality in preschool programs. Researchers have concluded that a teacher with a bachelor's degree in early childhood education is key to achieving positive outcomes for three- and four-year-olds.

8. Train parents to be stronger participants in their child's early learning. All preschool programs should include parent education. Research underscores the connection between the quality of a program and responsible parent involvement, showing that the more parents are involved, the better the chances that their children will succeed—just as in elementary school. Parents play an important role in program governance and need to be engaged as partners in their children's education. At the same time, school programs can support parents in setting and achieving their own goals for their child.

Beyond simply having a choice in where their child goes to school, parents must be empowered to be their child's most important teacher. Schools can help them to foster parent leadership skills, self-esteem and support their connection to community resources.

The National Association of Elementary School Principals and Collaborative Communications Group first teamed up in 2001 to produce the landmark publication *Leading Learning Communities: Standards for What Principals Should Know and Be Able To Do*. In 2004, NAESP again asked Collaborative Communications to conduct a rigorous examination of research; engage principals, researchers and individuals in professional organizations concerned with early childhood education; and write and design the companion guide *Leading Early Childhood Learning Communities*. The 10-month process included:

Focus groups. Principals and administrators at the Annual Professional Development Institute of the National Association for the Education of Young Children in June 2004 provided insight on effective strategies for connecting schools and early childhood programs and the significant transitions between home and preschool and preschool and school entry.

Discovery interviews. Thought leaders in research, policy and practice provided significant perspective regarding NAESP's role in the field of early childhood education. Interviews also provided important context about the importance of preschool in preparing children for school.

Creation and convening of an Early Childhood Standards Committee. Principals were nominated to the committee based on their excellence in early childhood education. These principals, along with individuals from early childhood professional organizations, helped to shape the guide, reviewing the research and approving the conceptual framework. The committee also provided examples of effective practice.

Scholarly research. A review of relevant research spanned return-on-investment and cost-benefit analyses, child outcome standards, early childhood development and brain research, leadership, teacher quality, physical environments, content and instruction, integration of schools and community services, parent and community collaboration, advocacy and federal, state and local policy.

Interviews with principals. Conversations with elementary school principals included those who had preschool programs in their buildings and those who did not. These conversations focused on effective practices, role of principals in supporting quality and integration of school and community preschool programs.

Discussion with the NAESP Board of Directors. The October 2004 board meeting provided an opportunity for reflection on the initial outline and fundamental messages of the guide.

Discussion with the National Distinguished Principals. The annual NDP celebration provided an opportunity for input and conversation among principals from all nine NAESP geographic zones.

Review of drafts. NAESP staff and leadership, Standards Committee members and external peers in early childhood professional organizations provided candid and invaluable feedback that helped to assure accuracy, credibility and meaningfulness.

Acknowledgments

NAESP gratefully acknowledges the individuals who contributed to the creation of this guide, including:

- The principals who participated in the NAEYC focus groups and on the Standards Committee; those who served as models of effective practice and are quoted in the guide and the National Distinguished Principals—all of whom provided important perspective on how the guide would be best utilized.

- The NAESP Board of Directors, listed below, for their commitment to calling to progressive practice and high-quality learning opportunities for all children.

- External reviewers including W. Steven Barnett, National Institute for Early Education Research; Libby Doggett, Pre-K Now; Shyrelle Eubanks, National Education Association; Peter Pizzolongo, National Association for the Education of Young Children; Diane Whitehead, National Head Start Association; and Edward Zigler, Center in Child Development and Social Policy at Yale University.

- Collaborative Communications Group staff and consultants, including Kris Kurtenbach and Terri Ferinde Dunham, Partners; Gloria Frazier, Senior Consultant; Lonnie Harp, Editor; Jeanne Jehl, Senior Consultant; Meghan Neary, Associate; Liz Worley, Copy Editor. Collaborative team members also included art direction and design by Bill Glover of DG Design Partners. Photographs by Bill Glover and Meghan Neary.

- Helene Segal-Turner, director of the Kensington Nursery School, for her contributions to this project.

- NAESP staff, for their commitment to providing research, professional development and expanded learning opportunities for elementary and middle school principals across the country, including:

Vincent L. Ferrandino, Ed.D., Executive Director; Gail Connelly Gross, Deputy Executive Director; Deborah B. Reeve, Ed.D., Deputy Executive Director; Cheryl Riggins Newby, Ed.D., Associate Executive Director, Leadership Academy and Urban Alliances; Fred Brown, Associate Executive Director, Membership Outreach, Professional Services and Principals Advisory Leadership Services Corps; Sally McConnell, Ph.D., Associate Executive Director, Government Relations; June Million, Director, Public Information; Merrie Hahn, Director, Programs; Diana Stanley, Coordinator, Executive Projects

Early Childhood Standards Committee

Rosemarie Young, Chair
Watson Lane Elementary School
7201 Watson Lane
Louisville, KY 40272

M. Sandra Allison-Harris
Belvedere Elementary School
6540 Columbia Pike
Falls Church, VA 20041

Elizabeth Carlson
Morris Early Childhood Center
8609 Third Street
Lincoln, DE 19960

Cheryl Downs
Columbia Elementary School
1502 Elm Street
P.O. Box 108
Rochester, IN 46975

Shyrelle Eubanks
National Education Association
1201 16th St, N.W.
Washington, DC 20036

Christine Frude
Paradise Valley School
22 Magnolia
Casper, WY 82604

Mike Garlough
Hunter-Tannerville Elementary School
7794 Main Street
Hunter, NY 12442

Vera Groover
Endeavor Primary Learning Center
2701 NW 56th Avenue
Lauderhill, FL 33313

Larry Kuper
Roy Elementary School
P.O. Box 238
Roy, WA 98580

Peter Pizzolongo
National Association for the Education
of Young Children
1509 16th Street, N.W.
Washington, DC 20036

Stacy Stoll
Greenridge Elementary School
3825 Oakridge
Comstock Park, MI 49321

Kathy Taber
Jefferson Elementary School
250 North Cockrel
Norman, OK 73071

Diane Whitehead
National Head Start Association
1651 Prince Street
Alexandria, VA 22314

Discovery Interviews

W. Steven Barnett, Director, National Institute for Early Education Research, New Brunswick, NJ

Julie Bosland, Director for Early Childhood and Family Economic Success, National League of Cities, Washington, DC

Barbara Bowman, President and Co-Founder, Erikson Institute and Chief Officer for Early Childhood Education, Chicago Public Schools, Chicago, IL

Libby Doggett, Executive Director, Pre-K Now, Washington, DC

Jill Flanders, Board Member, Strategies for Children, Boston, MA

Shyrelle Eubanks, Senior Professional Associate/Policy Analyst, National Education Association, Washington, DC

Marilou Hyson, Associate Executive Director for Professional Development, National Association for the Education of Young Children, Washington, DC

Lilian Katz, Co-Director, Clearinghouse on Early Education and Parenting, Champaign, IL

Lynn Mitchell, Policy Director, Corporate Voices for Working Families, Washington, DC

Carol Rasco, President and CEO, Reading Is Fundamental, Washington, DC

Deborah Stipek, Dean, Stanford University School of Education, Palo Alto, CA

Joseph Villani, Deputy Executive Director, National School Boards Association, Alexandria, VA

NAESP Board of Directors

President
Rosemarie I. Young
Watson Lane Elementary School
Louisville, KY

President-Elect
Susan Elizabeth Masterson
Monroe Elementary School
Janesville, WI

Past President
Anthony Harduar
Central Elementary School
Ferndale, WA

Director, Zone 1
Dana C. Folsom
San Carlos Park Elementary School
Fort Myers, FL

Director, Zone 2
Bonnie Lew Tryon
Golding Elementary School
Cobleskill, NY

Director, Zone 3
Nancy M. Davenport
Kingston Elementary School
Virginia Beach, VA

Director, Zone 4
Jack C. Meeds
Acreage Pines Elementary School
Loxahatchee, FL

Director, Zone 5
Paul J. Mikulcik
Mechanics Grove Elementary School
Mundelein, IL

Director, Zone 6
William J. Rich
McFall Elementary School
Middleville, MI

Director, Zone 7
Mary Kay Sommers
Shepardson Elementary School
Ft. Collins, CO

Director, Zone 8
Alan E. Michelson
Cordill-Mason Elementary School
Blue Springs, MO

Director, Zone 9
John S. Luher
Arlington Elementary School
Spokane, WA

Director, Foundation
Patrick D. Hould
Lewistown Junior High School
Lewistown, MT

Director, Foundation
Sherman A. LaPrade
Clays Mill Elementary School
Scottsburg, VA

Bibliography

STANDARD ONE: Embrace Early Childhood Learning

Barnett, W. Steven and Pamela J. Kelley, Eds. "Measuring Preschool Costs and Revenues: Issues and Answers. A Summary Report of the 2002 Early Education Cost Symposium." National Institute of Early Education Research, September 2002.

Belfield, C. R. "Research Briefing: The Pre-K Payback." Center for Early Care and Education, March 2004.

Bowman, B. T., M. S. Donovan and M. S. Burns, Eds. *Eager To Learn: Educating Our Preschoolers.* Washington, DC: National Academy Press, 2001.

Bruner, C. *A Stitch in Time: Calculating the Costs of School Unreadiness.* Washington, DC: The Finance Project, 2002.

Education Commission of the States. "Starting Early, Starting Now: A Policymaker's Guide to Early Care and Education and School Success." ECS, 2001.

Ferrandino, V. L. "Never Too Young To Learn." *Principal*, Vol. 80, No. 5. National Association of Elementary School Principals, May 2001.

Ferrandino, V. L. "Preschool Makes Perfect $ense." *Principals' Perspective.* National Association of Elementary School Principals, April 14, 2004.

Gershoff, E. "Low Income and the Development of America's Kindergarteners." *Living at the Edge* Research Brief, Vol. 4. National Center for Children in Poverty, November 2003.

National Association of Elementary School Principals. *Early Childhood Education and the Elementary School Principal: Standards for Quality Programs for Young Children*. Alexandria, VA: NAESP, 2nd edition, 1998.

National Research Council. *Eager To Learn: Educating Our Preschoolers*. Washington, DC: National Academy Press, 2001.

National Research Council and Institute of Medicine. *From Neurons to Neighborhoods: The Science of Early Childhood Development*. Washington, DC. National Academy Press, 2000.

Pfannenstiel, J.C., V. Seitz and E. Zigler. "Promoting School Readiness: The Role of the Parents as Teachers Program. *NHSA Dialog: A Research-to-Practice Journal for the Early Intervention Field*, Vol. 6, 2002.

Shore, Rima. *What Kids Need: Today's Best Ideas for Nurturing, Teaching and Protecting Young Children*. Boston, MA: Beacon Press, 2003.

Zigler, Edward. *Head Start and Beyond: A National Plan for Extended Childhood Intervention*. New Haven, CT: Yale University Press, 1995.

STANDARD TWO: Engage Families and Communities

Baker, Amy C., and Lynn Manfredi-Petitt. *Relationships, the Heart of Quality Care: Creating Community Among Adults in Early Care Settings*. Washington, DC: National Association for the Education of Young Children, 2004.

Dryfoos, Joy, and Sue Maguire. *Inside Full-Service Community Schools*. Thousand Oaks, CA: Corwin Press, 2002.

Epstein, Joyce L. School, *Family and Community Partnerships, Preparing Educators and Improving Schools*. Boulder, CO: Westview Press, 2001.

Lombardi, J. *Time To Care: Redesigning Child Care To Promote Education, Support Families and Build Communities*. Philadelphia, PA: Temple University Press, 2003.

National Center for Early Development and Learning. "Transition to Kindergarten." *National Center for Early Development and Learning*, Vol. 2, No. 2, Winter 2004.

Pianta, Robert and Marcia Kraft-Sayre. *Successful Kindergarten Transition, Your Guide to Connecting Children, Families and Schools*. Baltimore, MD: Brookes Publishing Company, 2003.

Takanishi, Ruby. "Leveling the Playing Field: Supporting Immigrant Children From Birth to Eight." *The Future of Children*, Vol. 14, No. 2.

STANDARD THREE: Promote Appropriate Learning Environments for Young Children

Bell, Susan Hart, Victoria W. Carr, Dawn Denno, Lawrence J. Johnson and Louise R. Phillips. *Challenging Behaviors in Early Childhood Settings: Creating a Place for All Children.* Baltimore, MD: Brookes Publishing Co., 2004.

Bredekamp, S. and Carol Copple, Eds. *Developmentally Appropriate Practice in Early Childhood Programs.* Washington, DC: National Association for the Education of Young Children, revised 1997.

Education Commission of the States and Knowledge Works Foundation. "Technology and Early Childhood Professional Development: A Policy Discussion." ECS and KWF, 2002.

Hemmeter, M. L., K. L. Maxwell, M. J. Ault and J. W. Schuster. *Assessment of Practices in Early Elementary Classrooms.* New York, NY: Teachers College Press, 2001.

National Association for the Education of Young Children. *Young Children*, Vol. 59, No. 4, July 2004.

Pate, Russell R., Karin A. Pfeiffer, Stewart G. Trost, Paula Ziefler, and Marsha Dowda. "Physical Activity Among Children Attending Preschools." *Pediatrics*, November 2004.

Smallwood, Diane. "Defusing Violent Behavior in Young Children." *Streamlined Seminar*, Vol. 21, No. 4. National Association of Elementary School Principals, Summer 2003.

Zigler, E. F., D. G. Singer and S. J. Bishop-Josef, Eds. *Children's Play: The Roots of Reading.* Washington, DC: Zero to Three Press, 2004.

STANDARD FOUR: Ensure Quality Teaching

American Association of Colleges for Teacher Education. "The Early Childhood Challenge: Preparing High-Quality Teachers for a Changing Society." AACTE, June 2004.

Barnett, W. S. "Better Teachers, Better Preschools: Student Achievement Linked to Teacher Qualifications." *Preschool Policy Matters*, Vol. 2. National Institute for Early Education Research, March 2003.

Collay, Michelle, Diane Dunlap, Walter Enloe and George W. Gagnon, Jr. *Learning Circles: Creating Conditions for Professional Development.* Thousand Oaks, CA, Corwin Press, 1998.

Coppedge, M. "When Does School Start? Should Kids Get on the Bus at Age Three?" *Endeavors Magazine*, Vol. 21, No. 1, Fall 2004.

"Early Childhood Curriculum and Assessment." *Scholastic Early Childhood Today*, Vol. 18, No. 6, April 2004.

Hyson, M., Ed. *Preparing Early Childhood Professionals: NAEYC's Standards for Programs.* Washington, DC: National Association for the Education of Young Children, 2003.

Katz, L. G. "Educating Young Children." *Streamlined Seminar*, Vol. 21, No. 3, National Association of Elementary School Principals, Spring 2003.

McMaken, J. "Early Childhood Assessment." *Early Learning Policy Brief.* Education Commission of the States, March 2003.

Neuman, S. B., C. Copple, and S. Bredekamp. *Learning To Read and Write: Developmentally Appropriate Practices for Young Children.* Washington, DC: National Association for the Education of Young Children, 2002.

Sornson, Bob, Ed. *Preventing Early Learning Failure.* Alexandria, VA: Association for Supervision and Curriculum Development, 2001.

Zigler, Edward and Sally J. Styfco, Eds. *The Head Start Debates.* New Haven, CT: Yale Center in Child Development and Social Policy, 2004.

STANDARD FIVE: Use Multiple Assessments To Strengthen Learning

Grace, C. and E. F. Shores. *The Portfolio Book: A Step-by-Step Guide for Teachers.* Beltsville, MD: Gryphon House, 1998.

McAfee, Oralie, Deborah J. Leong and Elena Bodrova. *Basics of Assessment: A Primer for Early Childhood Educators.* Washington, DC: National Association for the Education of Young Children, 2004.

Meisels, Samuel J. "Using Work Sampling in Authentic Assessments." *Educational Leadership*, Vol. 54, No. 4, December 1996/January 1997.

Sandall, Susan, Mary E. McLean and Barbara Smith. *DEC Recommended Practices in Early Intervention/Early Childhood Special Education.* Longmont, CO: Division for Early Childhood of the Council for Exceptional Children, 2000.

STANDARD SIX: Advocate for High-Quality, Universal Early Childhood Education

Committee for Economic Development. "Developmental Education: The Value of High Quality Preschool Investments as Economic Tools." CED, September 2004.

Committee for Economic Development. "Preschool For All: Investing in a Productive and Just Society." Committee for Economic Development, 2002.

Education Commission of the States. "Starting Early, Starting Now: A Policymaker's Guide to Early Care and Education and School Success." ECS, 2001.

Gormley, William T., Ted Guyer, Deborah Phillips and Brittany Dawson. "The Effects of Universal Pre-K in Oklahoma: Research Highlights and Policy Implications." Center for Research on Children in the United States Working Paper #2. Washington, DC: Georgetown University, 2004.